the Highland Coast

Orkney, Skye, Great Glen & Loch Ness

whisky route

ALASTAIR K. ROONEY

Spirit of the Glen

My Heart's in the Highlands

My Heart's in the Highlands,
 my heart is not here,
My Heart's in the Highlands,
 a-chasing the deer,
Chasing the wild-deer,
 and following the roe—
My Heart's in the Highlands,
 wherever I go!

—Robert Burns

Written by Alastair Rooney (akrooney1@outlook.com)

Published by Spirit of the Glen Ltd., Ilex House, 48 Ash Lane, Rustington, BN16 3BT • 07427 909906

Designed by Brad Brooks of Grafica by the Sea

This Guide is dedicated to my mother, Margaret (Peggy) Shaw born in Carron, near Cardhu. She lived her life in Inverness, a wonderful, dignified mother and lady (1921-2015)—Alastair Rooney

With special heartfelt thanks to my wife Sally and daughters, Sara and Emma for their continued support in my constant enthusiasm for projects of "folly". Grateful thanks to Liz and Brad of Grafica by the Sea for their support and guidance desperately needed by a "novice author". Sincere thanks to Jean Fraser and Pearl Rooney who were indispensable in Inverness and the Highlands. They both journeyed with me to experience the joys of the HC 700.

For those who "doubted"—I sincerely thank you – without the incentive of your doubts, I think I may have given-up, fallen and failed.

ISBN 978-1-9196252-0-1 • Print version

ISBN 978-1-9196252-1-8 • eBook version

the Highland Coast

whisky route

HC 700

Detours

To Inverness

Other Roads

Towns & Points of Interest

Ferry Routes

Contents

PICTURE CREDITS

Fiona Smeaton—fsmeaton@gmail.com
Adobe Stock—www.adobe.com/stock
iStock—www.istock.com
Shutterstock—www.shutterstock.com

Infographics & maps: Brad Brooks—brad@graficabythesea.com

Thistle–Cluaran

SECTION 1

Highland Coast (HC 700) Whisky Route

INVERNESS

The Capital and Gateway to the Northern Scottish Highlands is the start and finish location for the Highland Coast 700 Whisky Route.

The Highland Coast (HC 700) Whisky Route is more extensive than the NC 500 route in that the HC 700 includes visits to the Orkney Islands, Isle of Skye as well as the Great Glen and Loch Ness. The HC 700 Whisky Route Guide and the NC 500 use many of the same roads in the Region.

The HC 700 could also be used as a travel route guide *without the distillery visits*. It is an indispensable aid to planning your journey in the wild Highlands of Scotland.

The '700' relates to the estimated 700 miles on the Route. Please remember, the Route mileage is a personal choice, you can choose to skip parts of the Route and therefore travel shorter distances.

Some people choose to travel the HC 700 Whisky Route in different directions, West to East as opposed to the recommended East to West. Many consider completing this journey over several 3 day periods, whilst others take ten to fourteen days to complete the route.

Here are some examples:

Option 1—Inverness, Thurso and Orkney can be completed over three days. Some 110 miles to Thurso, then a car ferry crossing to Orkney (60 or 90 minutes) and then a road distance of just over 31 miles in Orkney. There is a choice of eight Whisky distilleries on this route.

Option 2—Inverness to Skye can be completed over two days. Travel 114 miles to Portree, with a choice of four Whisky distilleries.

Option 3—Inverness to Ullapool. These parts of the HC 700 can be visited over a 2-day period and covers approximately 114 miles. Two Distilleries on this route.

Whatever your choice, the HC 700 Whisky Route is waiting for you.

Before you start your HC 700 Whisky Route, it is vital to spend

some time planning your days, route, accommodation etc. This may seem a bit like homework, but the results from this or basic desk research can yield great dividends in terms of enjoyment, reduction of travel related stress and will contribute to a more wonderful experience. There are several other books, guides and maps that are important in the successful preparation for your whisky journey.

Discover the right distillery tours and tastings for you! A range of fascinating distilleries are available to educate the whisky novice, amateur or indeed the whisky connoisseur! Many distillery tours offer you the chance to indulge in tutored, professional tastings.

We hope this Whisky Guide reduces the number hours you spend on internet planning and guides you effortlessly on your tailor – made travel itinerary.

Here is a list of recommended reading for review, prior to your HC 700 journey. These books will greatly assist in the planning process.

ORDNANCE SURVEY (OS 1) ROAD MAP SHEET 1—NORTH SCOTLAND, ORKNEY & SHETLAND MAP

You will be tackling some difficult roads, particularly on the Northern and Western Coasts. Single track roads with passing places, heavily congested roads, lots of touring motorists perhaps not familiar with the local driving style. All combine to create a different and sometimes difficult driving experience. The summer months are particularly fraught with additional tourist traffic. It all points to the necessity of being well prepared in terms of the roads to be travelled. It is advisable that every evening you recap the next day's route and understand what stops and visitor experiences you may select in the miles to be covered. Day 4 and 5 are both serious driving days in terms of distance and the poor quality and infrastructure of the roads. This will be offset and compensated by the stunning Western Coast scenery, which is truly magnificent. So, purchase an OS Map 1. It does not include Skye, so you will also need a good quality map of the Skye. OS Map 1 will be your route 'bible', so remember to have it with you in the car, hotel or just have it readily available to discuss the HC 700 Whisky Route with any other interested people you meet.

GRIDREFERENCEFINDER.COM

This is an absolutely vital website to preview prior to and also to have available during your trip. The website can convert Grid References to Postal / Sat. Nav. Codes or to Latitude /Longitude readings. It cleverly allows you to 'drive' the road at home and provides greater details on the route. Try this on the route from Durness to Ullapool. As you 'drive' the route you can see the names of the lochs and other features you will be passing, plus the other scenic beauties to look out for on your journey.

SCOTCH WHISKY

A good understanding of this important subject matter is fundamental. So, purchase a well compiled and written book on the subject of Scotch whisky. Charles Maclean is an excellent choice of author. His 'nose' is second to none in the whisky business. Razor sharp prose compliments his acumen in sniffing out the finest whiskies. One of his many books on whisky should be your second 'bible'. Keep this by your bedside, in the car or simply as an information companion. Yes–the internet is great, but Charlie is better on the topic of malt whisky. His books, Malt Whisky - The Complete Guide and Whiskypedia.

THE NORTH COAST 500 GUIDE BOOK BY CHARLES TAIT

An excellent companion on the HC 500 route. Every conceivable fact you would wish to know about the

Northern Highlands is contained within the pages of his authoritative guide. An extremely effective way to understand the history, geography and infrastructure of this wonderful part of Scotland. The NC 500 travels along many of the same roads as the HC 700 Whisky Route. The HC 700 Whisky Route includes the Islands of Orkney, Isle of Skye, the Great Glen and Loch Ness. These are not included in the NC 500. In his 256 pages guide, Charles shows he is truly a literary giant amongst his peers in the presentation of an astounding amount of factual information and amazing photos of the Highlands.

RAW SPIRIT: IN SEARCH OF THE PERFECT DRAM BY IAIN BANKS

A light read, Banks, (of The Wasp Factory fame) was commissioned to write this fascinating book. Light-hearted,humorous and passionate, as only a Scotsman can write about his native country, the national drink and his fellow Scots. Sadly, Iain passed away in 2013. He wrote in the forward to his book 'Everything in here is true. Especially the bits I made up'! Ian Rankin writes a wonderful introduction about the author and his book. A fitting tribute. Did Iain find the perfect dram? You will need to read the book to find out.

THE HC 700 WHISKY GUIDE

Designed to be used as a 6-day guide. The number of days and routes chosen are a personal preference. The HC 700 is a stunning scenic route, so time should be taken to stop and view the natural beauty, haunting glens, moors, mountains, lochs and the wild coasts.

The above books are all readily available from Amazon or any good bookshop.

Each day has a route map with Points of Interest (POI), distilleries and the proposed overnight stop. Information is shown on recommended cafes, restaurants, whisky bars and shops.

Day 1—Inverness and its historical surroundings. One distillery visit is available on this day.

Day 2—Inverness to Wick, with a choice of four excellent distilleries.

Day 3—A visit to the Orkney Islands. This involves a ferry crossing from either Gills Bay or Scrabster to Orkney. Orkney has two superb whisky distilleries. A choice of three distilleries on this day.

Day 4—A driving day that includes some of the most spectacular coastal scenery in the world. No distillery visits on this day.

Day 5—From Ullapool, cross the Skye Bridge at Kyle of Lochalsh on to the Isle of Skye. A possible option to visit the two Skye whisky distilleries. A long day and driving journey. Consider an additional overnight stop if you are concerned about distance and time.

Day 6—Return to Inverness, this involves one distillery visit and a drive along part of the magnificent Great Glen, and the shores of Loch Ness. You will be able to visit the Loch Ness Monster Museum Centre and the historic Glen Urquhart Castle.

Your personal agenda on the 6-day route can be varied to suit your specific touring wishes. Feel free to reduce the distance or opt out of Skye or Orkney. The journey and the fascinating routes are more important than the destination.

The HC 700 Whisky Guide details all the relevant roads you will travel on and it also provides postal codes for all the places you may wish to visit. We suggest you contact your chosen distilleries and whisky shops at the planning stage and most definitely prior to arriving. Many whisky tours or tastings must be booked in advance.

In addition to the distillery visitor shops, we have recommended independent whisky shops where you can sample a wider range of other regional Scottish whiskies.

Chauffeur driven itineraries and the hire of a six or eight seat minibus are available from Inverness. It is possible to arrange an organised bus

> ***If you are very fortunate you may be lucky to view the wonder of the Northern Lights or Aurora Borealis. Seen mostly on the Northern and Western coasts. Usually witnessed in the latter part of the evening or night. A celestial dance of multi-coloured lights across the night sky. Truly spectacular!***

tour from Inverness, but this will have a defined itinerary of distilleries and places to be visited.

Remember, if you are driving, Scotland's laws on drinking and driving are stricter than the rest of the UK or many places in Europe. Penalties include a mandatory minimum driving ban of 12 months, a fine of up to £5000, and in serious cases, up to six months in prison.

The limits are as follows:

	Scotland	Rest of UK
Micrograms per 100ml of breath	22	35

If you are offered sample whisky in distilleries then take some empty 5 cl sample bottles with you and drink the distillery whisky samples in the evening at your accommodation. Some distilleries will be happy to provide samples in whisky bottles.

If you have chosen to participate in the HC 700 Whisky Route passport, please remember to obtain your HC 700 stamps along the route. Many outlets such as hotels, restaurants, whisky bars and tourist shops have the HC Whisky 700 stamp. If not, simply obtain a signature, name and address of any distillery, or other outlets on the Whisky Route.

Do not forget to take copious, memorable photographs and if you choose to, forward your photos to the HC 700 website for public display.

Now you are ready for the journey of a lifetime. Please have a wonderful time and do not hesitate to contact us if you require any further assistance.

turas math dhut!

(Scots Gaelic for *'a good journey to you'* or Bon Voyage)

SECTION 2

Travel Options to Inverness and Transport en route

TRAVEL TO INVERNESS

Inverness is readily accessible by road, rail and air.

ROAD

The *A90*, *M90* and *A9* from Edinburgh, the *A82* from Glasgow or the *A96* from Aberdeen, all provide direct access to Inverness via the east or west coast. However, in the summer months these roads are heavily congested with lorries, cars, caravans, motor-cycles and motor homes. During winter months, these roads can be fraught and dangerous with frequent heavy rain, snow and icy conditions.

RAIL

Inverness railway station provides direct access from London. The day-time service and the Caledonian Sleeper train departs from Euston, London on a daily schedule. The travel time to Inverness from London is approximately 10.00 hours. There are also direct rail services from Edinburgh, Aberdeen and Glasgow and all railway stations from the South of Scotland and England. The railway line also extends northwards to Wick and Thurso.

AIR

Dalcross Airport (Inverness). The airport is some nine miles from Inverness. Many airlines such as EasyJet, British Airways and Jet 2 use the airport. Flights connect with Heathrow, Gatwick, Bristol, Birmingham, Manchester, Luton, Belfast and Leeds. Air travel time from London is approximately 1hr 40mins. International flights from Amsterdam and Dublin.

TRANSPORT ON THE HC 700 WHISKY ROUTE

- *Private Car*
- *Hire cars, Minibuses, or 4x4 SUVs* are all available
- *Motorcycles:* Hire bikes are available

- *Caravans:* extreme care must be taken on the narrower roads especially those on the north west sector. Smaller caravans are most definitely recommended
- *Motorhomes:* extreme care must be taken and smaller units are more preferable
- *Welcome to Inverness Taxis::* A company that provides safe travel in Inverness and Scotland with a team of highly-experienced drivers. Offering a professional transport service where your safety and satisfaction are paramount. A friendly and reliable taxi service. We support safe transfer (SAFEKAB), personalised Highland Tours, executive and private car hire, with airport transfers. Wheelchair access. E-bike hire. IT Tours & Drinks, 55 Church St, Inverness IV1 1DR *01463 222222* *www.inverness-taxis.com*

HIRE OF A CAR, MOTORCYCLE OR A MOTORHOME

- *Rental cars* can be collected from Dalcross Airport or Inverness City Centre. A wide selection of car hire companies is available.
- *Motorcycle hire:* A range of motorcycles can be hired, inc. Harleys. **Haggis Tours** is based in Tore some 8 miles outside Inverness IV6 7RY. *01463 800041*
- *Motorhome Hire:* **Coast to Glen Motorhomes** provide a range of motorhomes for hire—delivery can be arranged. They are based in Inverness IV4 7JQ. *01463 741639*

WILD CAMPING

A real growth area with many peoples wishing to be closer to nature. Scotland's relaxed land laws allows wild camping in many open areas. Please leave the site exactly as you found it. Respect local customs and remove all your litter and rubbish.

DAY ONE MAP – INVERNESS TO TOMATIN

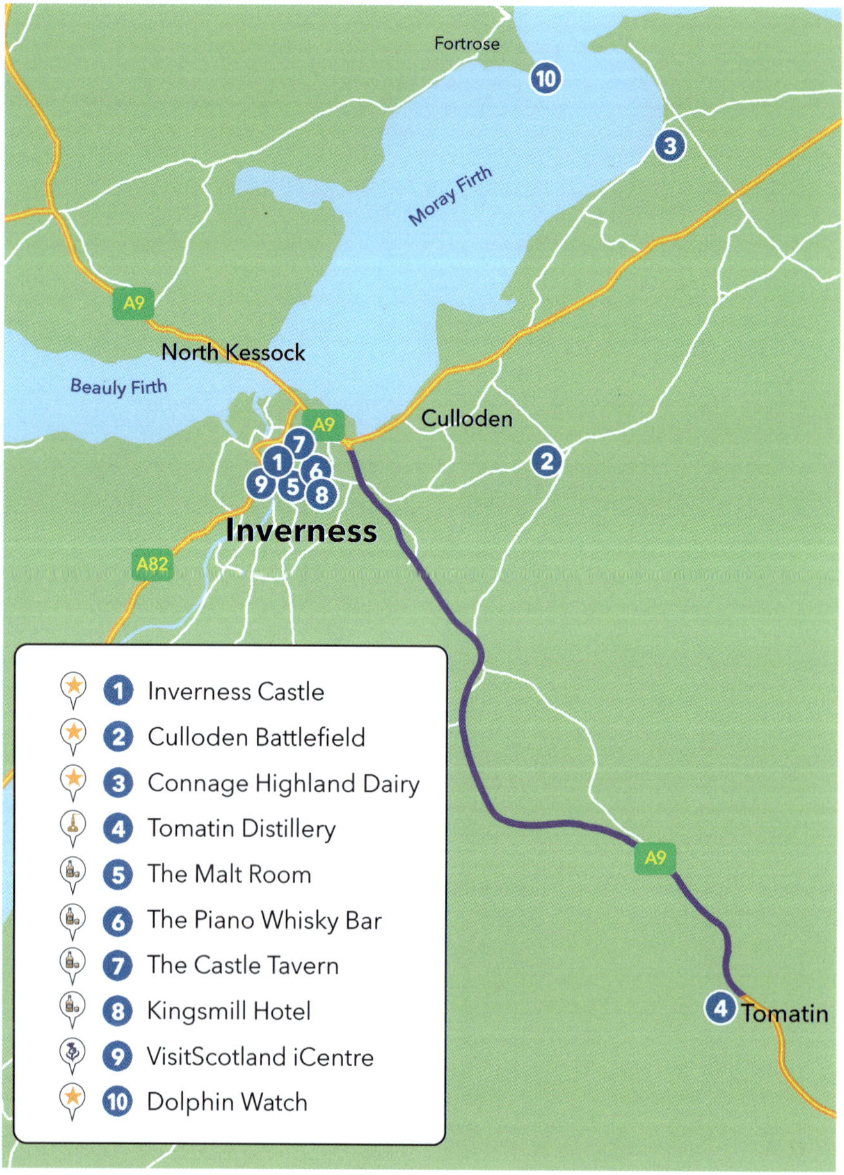

SECTION 3

Day One
Inverness

WELCOME TO THE SCOTTISH HIGHLANDS

We recommend using the East to West HC 700 Coastal route.

This involves travelling north from Inverness, up the East Coast, crossing the top coast of Northern Scotland and then travelling down south on the West Coast and finally return East to Inverness. This route permits visits to a choice of distilleries on days 1,2,3,5 and 6.

The Route can also be travelled in the opposite direction - West to East Coast. It is a personal choice, but we prefer to leave the magnificent scenery of the West Coast to the last days!

Accommodation and distillery visits should be booked before departing for the route.

The HC 700 Route is best completed in the summer months when the hours of daylight are much longer (day light up to 22.00 in the height of summer).

Shown below are the important map signs and symbols for your whisky journey:

- **Point of Interest, a road change or an important junction**
- **Whisky Bars/Shops**
- **Distillery**
- **Seafood/Shellfish Restaurants**
- **Highland Game and Scottish Produce Restaurant**
- **Cafés and Bistros**
- **Recommended Fish & Chips with a special location**
- **Visit Scotland iCentres**

INVERNESS

Flora Macdonald

A visit to Inverness Castle is highly recommended. Parking around the Castle is limited, but parking is available at the Eastgate Shopping Centre with only a short stroll along the pedestrianised High Street. The tourist information centre, Visit Scotland i Centre is on the High Street. Castle views along the River Ness are scenic, looking toward Ben Wyvis, to the extinct volcano at Craig Phadrig. It is believed St. Columba visited here in 565 AD to meet King Brude. It is also believed that Craig Phadrig was the site of Macbeth's Castle.

Do not forget to stop at the statue of Flora Macdonald, located in front of the Castle. Stroke her statue crest before departing. Hopefully, this will ensure good luck and fortune on your HC 700 journey. She certainly brought good luck to Bonnie Prince Charlie in 1746 as he escaped after the failure of the Jacobite Rising. It is claimed he dressed as Flora's maid to escape the Government soldiers. Flora with her border collie is looking to the west, along the Great Glen and onwards to the Isle of Skye and the Outer Hebrides.

The Castle Tavern (opposite the entrance to the Castle) is a great place to start your journey, have a coffee, breakfast or a meal. They will also provide your first HC 700 stamp, if you are completing the HC 700 Whisky Route Passport.

THE BATTLEFIELD OF CULLODEN IV2 5EU

The battlefield of Culloden is some 9 miles from Inverness and is a National Trust for Scotland Heritage site. Details of the clan positions and burial grounds are shown in the impressive Visitor Centre. This includes a video presentation and a visit to the actual battlefield locations of the Clans. This was the last battle fought on British soil—16th April,1746.

BOAT TOURS ON LOCH NESS, IV3 8JG

01463 233999

Consider a boat cruising trip on the Caledonian Canal and Loch Ness. ***BEWARE OF NESSIE!***

The departure pier is on the outskirts of Inverness on the A82 at Dochgarroch Lock.

DOLPHIN WATCH, ECOVENTURES, IV11 8YE ☎ 01381 600323

Bottlenose dolphins

Another great boat trip option is dolphin spotting from Cromarty Firth, some 16 miles from Inverness. Best location for bottlenose dolphin sightings in the UK. You can also view the dolphins from the shore. The site crosses a local golf course - Chanonry Point, Fortrose, IV10 8SD.

KILTMAKERS • HIGHLAND HOUSE OF FRASER, 4-9 HUNTLEY ST, IV1 1DR ☎ 01463 222781

Ever thought of owning a kilt? Choose your tartan; kilts can be handmade or off the peg. Visit the shop for the unique Scottish kiltmaker visitor experience with the finest hand-stitched kilts.

CONNAGE HIGHLAND DAIRY ARDERSIER, IV2 7QU ☎ 01667 462000

A truly magnificent cheese dairy some 10 miles from Inverness. Cheese made freshly on the farm overlooking the Moray Firth. Shop, dairy viewings and product courier service available.

JOHN M. MUNRO LTD., 22-24 QUEENSGATE, IV1 1DJ ☎ 01463 233066

The best Highland meat and game, from an award-winning butcher. They will vacuum pack and courier product, if you wish to take or send home.

From	**Inverness**
To	**Tomatin**
Road	**A9**
Miles	**30**
Time	**46 minutes**

DISTILLERY 1
TOMATIN DISTILLERY INVERNESS, IV13 7YT

The first distillery experience of your journey could be a visit to the Tomatin Distillery, which is just off the A9, some 16 miles south of Inverness. Continuing south on the A9 would take you into the Cairngorm National Park. Tomatin Distillery sits high in the Monadhliath Mountains, in an area of peat bogs and wild windy moorland with magnificent views of the Cairngorms to the south.

It is possible to Visit Culloden Moor when travelling on the A9.

THE TOMATIN DISTILLERY

01463 248144 • visitors@tomatin.com
https://www.tomatin.com

The unique legacy of Tomatin began in 1897. Take a tour and sample three expressions of their malt whisky or purchase your own bottle of single cask malt whisky. The Tomatin Distillery is home to Tomatin, a world renowned and award winning Highland single malt; Cù Bòcan, a subtly smoky and surprisingly sweet single malt that explores innovative finishes; and The Antiquary, a premium blend crafted with only the finest and rarest malts. Tomatin is one of the highest distilleries in the UK and is owned by the Japanese company, Takara Shuzo.

The Legacy Tour

Over 18s—£10 • Under 18s—£4
Allow 1 hr 15 mins

Booking is strongly advised
Enjoy your visit
Tlachd as do chuairt

Overnight stay in Inverness

Inverness has several excellent whisky bars, superb restaurants with Highland cuisine and a wide range of accommodation options.

WHISKY BARS

THE MALT ROOM, 34 CHURCH STREET, IV1 1EH • 01463 221888

300 different whiskies are available for tasting. They offer whiskies in the Modest, Memorable and Magnificent categories as well as whisky 'flights'.

THE WHISKY BAR, THE KINGSMILL HOTEL, CULCABOCK RD, IV2 3LP 01463 237166

Over 100 whiskies stocked in the bar.

THE PIANO AND WHISKY BAR, GLENMORISTON TOWN HOUSE HOTEL, 20 NESS BANK, IV2 4SF 01463 233777

Over 260 malts in stock.

FAT BUDDA, 19 YOUNG ST, IV3 5TT
01463 232889

Fish & Chips with a Chinese option. Superb with the option of a stroll along the banks of the River Ness. Memorable...

THE CASTLE TAVERN, 1 VIEW PLACE, IV2 4SA. • 01463 718178

A traditional Real Ale and whisky bar, restaurant and garden. Look out for 'Malt of the Month'.

PERK COFFEE & DOUGHNUTS, 36 CHURCH ST. IV1 1EH • 01463 718178

Next to the Malt Room Whisky Bar, Perk serves delicious barista coffee and unique hand-made doughnuts. They have a range of breakfast & lunch takeaways, with vegan options available. As a special treat, try the whisky doughnuts—magic!

VISIT SCOTLAND INVERNESS I CENTRE

36 High Street, Inverness, IV1 1JQ
01463 252401

Notes

DAY TWO MAP – INVERNESS TO WICK

SECTION 4

Day Two
Inverness to Wick

A PLETHORA OF DISTILLERIES TO CHOOSE!

There are four wonderful distilleries to choose from on this day. All with whisky tasting and distillery tours.

A difficult choice, so please do your research and maximise your HC 700 whisky experience. Remember to consider whisky tastings as opposed to distillery operational visits. The tasting-only option will allow you to visit a larger number of distilleries.

From	Inverness
To	Alness
Road	A9
Miles	23
Time	30 minutes

Drive out of Inverness, following the signs for the A9 North, passing over the Kessock Bridge with great views of the Beauly and Moray Firth. The Black Isle (not an island) is on the right. At the Tore roundabout, take the A9 to Thurso/Wick.

Continue along the A9 towards the Cromarty Firth. Cross the Cromarty Firth Bridge and head towards Alness whilst enjoying impressive views of the Firth. On the A9 you will see the signs for the Dalmore Distillery.

DISTILLERY 2
DALMORE DISTILLERY
ALNESS, IV17 0UT

DALMORE DISTILLERY

01349 882362
enquiries@thedalmore.com
https://www.thedalmore.com

Beginning with the perfectly, stunning, riverside location, on the banks of The Cromarty Firth, this North Highland setting is where the Dalmore takes its name; 'The Dalmore', literally meaning 'Big Meadow'. The Dalmore distillery was established in 1839 by Alexander Matheson. Our 12 point Royal stag tells the story of King Alexander III, who was saved from a charging stag by Colin of Kintail, Chief of the Clan MacKenzie. Since 1867, The Dalmore has proudly carried the 12 point Royal Stag on each and every bottle; a marker for exceptional quality and a lasting testament to our Royal Heritage.

Tour Details

Three different tours and tastings are available. Guests must be at least 8 years old. *Monday to Thursday* 10.00 to 16.30. *Friday* 10.00 to 15.00. Group bookings by appointment at weekends. Small visitor shop.

Enjoy your visit

Tlachd as do chuairt

From	**Alness**
To	**Tain**
Road	**A9**
Miles	**15**
Time	**19 minutes**

Leave Alness and travel along the Cromarty Firth to Tain. On your right you will see Nigg Bay, and possibly some oil rigs, berthed at the disused oil rig fabrication plant.

On the A9, just after Tain, you will see the welcoming sign for The Glenmorangie Distillery.

DISTILLERY 3
GLENMORANGIE DISTILLERY
TAIN, IV19 1PZ

GLENMORANGIE DISTILLERY

01862 892477
tain-shop@glenmorangie.com
https://www.glenmorangie.com

GLENMORANGIE
SINGLE MALT SCOTCH WHISKY

Enter our Highland world, where all tastes are possible. Swirling with aroma and flavour, the Glenmorangie Distillery is the beating heart of our wondrous whisky creation.

Here you will meet the Distillers of Tain. Deeply versed in our anything-is-possible style of whisky making, these men and women possess skills built over generations. Truth be told, we couldn't create our delicious whiskies without them.

Discover our world by immersing yourself in the art of our whisky making. In the company of our passionate guides, see how we use barley, water, wood and time to bottle the taste of our imagination.

The distillery was first licenced in 1843 and is famous for its exciting and experimental use of different, exotic oak casks for maturation. The water comes from the Tarlogie

Springs and their pot stills are the tallest in Scotland. Affectionately known as " Giraffes " Unusually, the water used is rich in minerals; some say this is part of the unique flavour.

Glenmorangie is the biggest selling malt whisky in the UK. How to pronounce Glenmorangie correctly? *'Glen—m—orangey'*.

Tour Details

Classic Tasting 10:30 & 1:30, Innovator Tasting 12pm & 3pm. Tours will restart when COVID restrictions ease. It is also possible to visit the Tasting Room without a distillery visit. Advance booking is highly recommended. Open 10.00 to 17.00 *Monday to Friday*. Best method for booking is via the online form on the website or by emailing the above address.

Enjoy your visit

Tlachd as do chuairt

Just outside Tain is the Balblair Distillery which is accessed via the A9 and then the A836. *Take care to drive on the A836 before crossing the Dornoch Firth bridge.*

DISTILLERY 4
BALBLAIR DISTILLERY
EDDERTON, TAIN, IV19 1LB

BALBLAIR DISTILLERY

01862 821273
onlineshop@interbevgroup.com
https://www.balblair.com

Balblair is claimed to be the one of the oldest distillery in Scotland. The founding of the distillery is said to be in 1790. The Distillery has had long associations with the Ross family and Clan. On the distillery doorstep is the Clach Biorach, a four thousand year-old Pictish standing stone. On this prehistoric stone you will see a Pictish carving of a Z-rod, believed to represent the passage of time.

The single malt whisky is unpeated but there is a slight 'peated' presence which comes from the local burn (stream) Ault Dearg. Balblair comes with a light taste and is presented in an unusually shaped whisky bottle. Single malt whisky sold at 46% ABV. The distillery owner is Inver House Distillers; now part of Pacific Spirit (UK) Ltd, and subsequently owned by the InterBev Group.

Tour Details

Tours are available 10.00 to 16.00 - *Monday to Friday*. Three types of tour available including the *'Angel's Share'* tasting. Shop available for product and merchandise. Visitors can buy their own bottle from a hand-selected cask. Even filling, corking and sealing it yourself. You will have captured you own slice of True Highland Spirit!

Enjoy your visit

Tlachd as do chuairt

Return to the A9; Time permitting, a slight detour on the A949 to Dornoch is certainly worthwhile. Even perhaps, a round of golf at Royal Dornoch Golf Club!

From	**Tain**
To	**Dornoch**
Road	**A9**
Miles	**10**
Time	**15 minutes**

A949

Take this road to detour to Dornoch.

DORNOCH CASTLE HOTEL AND WHISKY BAR, CASTLE STREET, IV25 3SD

01862 810216

An upscale castle converted into a fine hotel. Award-winning whisky bar. Voted top whisky bar in many surveys. It is regarded as one of the finest whisky bars in Scotland. Splendid selection of vintage malts and rare bottling. The family owned hotel has added a micro distillery in the grounds.

Whisky tastings at the hotel are available but must be pre-booked.

CARNEGIE WHISKY CELLARS

IV25 3FD

01862 811791

An award-winning whisky shop with hugely knowledgeable staff. Wonderful selection of fine and aged whiskies. Personal tastings by advance booking. *HC 700 Whisky passport stamp is available here.*

ROYAL DORNOCH GOLF CLUB

IV25 3LW

01862 810219

Golf since 1616. This is one of the finest championship courses in

Scotland. Many golfers delight in

playing this links course, which is one of the top 10 courses in the world.

From	**Dornoch**
To	**Brora**
Road	**A949, A9**
Miles	**18**
Time	**24 minutes**

GOLSPIE

Look for the Dunrobin signs.

DUNROBIN CASTLE & GARDENS

GOLSPIE, KW10 6SF
01408 633177
WWW.DUNROBINCASTLE.CO.UK

A stately home and the family seat of the Earl of Sutherland. Completed in 1845. Open to the public, they host a stunning falconry display along with other birds of prey. Magnificent gardens with a coffee and visitor shop.

Continue on the A9 and just out of Brora, follow the signs for the Clynelish Distillery, Brora. Clynelish is on the left-hand side of the A9, signposted Clynelish Road Balnocoil or the C1098. The last opportunity for a distillery visit on your second day.

DISTILLERY 5
CLYNELISH DISTILLERY, KW10 6LR

CLYNELISH DISTILLERY

01408 623000 • clynelish@malts.com
https://www.malts.com

The distillery first opened in 1819. The proximity to the seashore gives a faint salty flavour, more associated with island malts. Other distilleries are closer to the coast, but they do not show this marine characteristic. A dried fruit and slightly smoky flavour, with a dry finish. Note the Scottish wild cat on the label. Located near the shores of the Dornoch Firth, and originally built in 1819 by the Marquess of Stafford. A replacement distillery was built in 1968. 'Ours is a craft not a process'. The distillery is owned by Diageo.

Tour Details

New Visitor Centre open. Please contact directly for available tours.

Enjoy your visit

Tlachd as do chuairt

The Highland Coast (HC 700) Whisky Route

From	Brora
To	Wick
Road	A9, A99
Miles	47
Time	1h 12m

TIMESPAN
HELMSDALE, KW8 6JA

Local history museum. Displays the historical effects of the Highland clearances.

LATHERON

Take the A99 road to Wick, taking in the amazing sea views.

Daily Total	113 Miles	2h 38m

Overnight stop at Wick

SHORTEST STREET IN THE WORLD
EBENEZER PLACE, WICK, KW1 5EA

As seen in the *Guinness Book of Records*, Ebenezer Place is a total of 2.06m long!

WICK MARINA & HARBOUR
KW1 5EN
01955 602030

An 80 berth marina just 5 minutes from the town centre.

MACKAYS BAR & NO.1 BISTRO,
MACKAYS HOTEL, WICK KW1 5ED
01955 602323 (BAR)
01955 602030 (BISTRO)

A great range of whiskies are available—500 in fact. Staff have a wide knowledge and are always willing to assist in choosing a malt whisky just for you. Private tastings are possible and must be pre-booked. The Mackay Hotel also offers accommodation with whisky packages. The bar is next to the shortest street in the world according to the *Guinness Book of Records*, Ebenezer Place. The staff at the hotel will gladly point you in the correct direction!

BORD DE L'EAU
2 MARKET STREET KW1 4AR
01955 604400

Great French restaurant and superb seafood.

HARBOUR CHIP SHOP, KW1 5EN
01955 604400

Best fish & chips takeaway and location.

VISIT SCOTLAND WICK I CENTRE

Norseman Hotel, Riverside, Wick, KN1 4NL. 01845 2255121

DAY THREE MAP – WICK AND THE ORKNEY ISLANDS

SECTION 5

Day Three
Wick & the Orkney Islands

A CHOICE TO MAKE...

Today, you will have to decide whether you wish to visit the Orkney Islands or travel directly on to Ullapool.

Start day 3 with a tour of the Old Pulteney Distillery close to the old harbour.

DISTILLERY 8
OLD PULTERNEY DISTILLERY
KW1 5BA

OLD PULTENEY DISTILLERY

01955 602371 • tfraser@inverhouse.com
https://www.oldpulteney.com

Defined and shaped by its stunning coastal location, Old Pulteney single malt Scotch whisky owes much to its home town of Wick. Established in 1826 at a time when the town was a thriving fishing port. Wick was known for it's barrels of Silver Darlings (herring) and Golden barrels of whisky. Old Pulteney has a strong place in the heart and history of this coastal community. Old Pulteney captures the taste of the sea in every drop of its liquid gold; from subtle coastal chords to more defined salty notes.

Tour Details

Tours available on *Monday* to *Friday* from 10.00 to 16.00.
Purchase your own hand – filled bottle from the cask collection. An excellent tour with an interesting Visitor Centre showing the fascinating history of Old Pulteney. Shop with merchandise on site.

Enjoy your visit

Tlachd as do chuairt

From	**Wick**
To	**John o'Groats**
Road	**A99**
Miles	**18**
Time	**23 minutes**

CASTLE SINCLAIR GIRNIGOE
KW1 4QT

Castle Sinclair

From Wick, head toward Noss Head on an un-signposted, small road that leads to the castle. Some 3 miles north of Wick. A short walk to the castle ruins with a car park close by. Many explanatory signs on the site to explain the history of the castle. Dramatic photo opportunity. Noss Head lighthouse visible from the coast.

John o' Groats is famous as the northern end of the UK journey which starts in Land's End, Cornwall. The John o' Groats signpost showing multiple destinations and is an iconic photo opportunity - the sign is taken down every evening! The town is named after Dutchman Jan de Groot, who established a ferry crossing to the Orkneys in the 11th Century. He charged one 'groat' for the crossing.

John O'Groats

DUNCANSBY HEAD
KW1 4YS

Superb Lighthouse. On the C1061 road, east of John o' Groats. Turn off onto Duncansby Head Road. The spectacular nearby sea stacks are also very photogenic.

The Pentland Firth is famous for the strength of its tides, which are among the fastest in the world; a speed of 18 miles per hour (16 knots) being reported west of Pentland Skerries. The force of the tides gives rise to overfalls and tidal races which can occur at different stages of the tide. Combined with gale force winds, they often give rise to extremely violent sea conditions.

The first recorded swim across the Pentland Firth was by Colleen Blair in 2011.

Orkney is an island archipelago with a Viking heritage, famous for its seals and seabirds.

There are two wonderful and expressive whisky distilleries on the Orkney Islands.

Car ferry trips to the Orkney Islands are available throughout the year. These depart from either Gills Bay or Scrabster. However, the Pentland Firth's treacherous reputation means crossings are dependent on the sea conditions. Therefore please try to include this factor into your planning. You will need to decide which ferry crossing you wish to take. Full details on the ferry options are shown below. As always, booking in advance is absolutely essential. Consider taking one ferry there and the other ferry on the return journey.

From	**John o'Groats**
To	**Gills Bay**
Road	**A836**
Miles	**3**
Time	**5 minutes**

CAR FERRY OPTIONS

FERRY OPTION 1

PENTLAND FERRIES, GILLS BAY, KW1 4YB
0800 688 8998
SALES@PENTLANDFERRIES.CO.UK
WWW.PENTLANDFERRIES.CO.UK

From Gills Bay to St. Margaret's Hope, Orkney.

The ferry departs for St. Margaret's Hope, with three crossings per day. Crossing time is approximately 60 minutes. It is advisable to book in advance online.

Car ferry rate is *£40* per crossing (not including driver or passengers).

Motorcycle ferry rate is *£18* per crossing (not including the driver or passenger).

Motorhome or caravan (up to 5m) ferry rate is *£40* per crossing (not including driver or passengers).

ISLAND OF STROMA

Colonies of seabirds, including puffins, gannets and many others bird species as well as seals and possibly dolphins.

Puffins

HOXA HEAD

The abandoned gun fort at Hoxa Head is visible from the Penland ferry.

SACPA FLOW

Britain's chief naval base until 1956. Great diving location because of the scuttled naval warships.

From	**St. Margaret's Hope**
To	**Kirkwall**
Road	**A961**
Miles	**16**
Time	**24 minutes**

OR this route if no ferry:

From	**John o'Groats**
To	**Scrabster**
Road	**A836**
Miles	**20**
Time	**28 mins** (only if NorthLink Ferry is used both ways)

DUNNET HEAD

If you choose to travel on the NorthLink Ferry, a visit to Dunnet Head (some seven miles from John o' Groats) is worthwhile. It is the UK's most northerly mainland point, not John o' Groats. Wonderful sea views across the Pentland Firth towards Orkney.

FERRY OPTION 2

NORTHLINK FERRIES
SCRABSTER FERRY TERMINAL, QUEEN ELIZABETH PIER, KW14 7UT
0800 111 4422
INFO@NORTHLINKFERRIES.CO.UK
WWW.NORTHLINKFERRIES.CO.UK

Sailings from Scrabster to Stromness, Orkney.

Crossing time is approximately 90 minutes and there are three crossings per day.

Northlink Ferry

Car ferry rates are between £57 to £63 per crossing, depending on the season.

Motorcycle ferry rates are between £16.80 and £21.25 per crossing, depending on the season.

Motorhome or caravan (under 6m) ferry rates are between £57 to £63 per crossing, depending on the season. The Magnus Premium Lounge is available for £7.50 per crossing. Good value.

TO SEE FROM THE FERRY

A wide range of seabirds, seals and possibly dolphins.

THE OLD MAN OF HOY

The Old Man of Hoy sea stack is visible from the ferry.

Old Man of Hoy

From	**Stromness**
To	**Kirkwall**
Road	**A965**
Miles	**15**
Time	**21 minutes**

SKARA BRAE PREHISTORIC VILLAGE

KW16 3LR
01856 841815

Europe's best-preserved settlement dating back to 3000 BC. Ruins of eight houses with a modern Visitor Centre (on the A967 and B9055).

RING OF BRODGAR, KW16 3JZ
01856 841815

A dramatic upright stone circle monument dating back to the Neolithic period (on the B9055 road off the A965).

DISTILLERY 7
HIGHLAND PARK DISTILLERY
HOLM ROAD, KW15 1SU

HIGHLAND PARK DISTILLERY

01856 874619
tours@highlandparkwhisky.com
https://www.highlandparkwhisky.com

Highland Park is on the A965 at Holm Road. The distillery was founded in 1798. The distillery is proud of the Islands Viking heritage. Floor malting of barley continues in the distillery, one of the few distilleries to continue this historical technique. Two operational kilns are used to hand turn the malted barley with hand cut peat. Highland Park has a resonant smoky tone and shows a slightly creamy texture. Peat is taken from nearby Hobbister Moor and adds to the depth and character. Peat is normally harvested in April. Highland Park is also unique in that it works with managed forests and then sends the oak staves to Jerez in Spain for manufacture into sherry casks. These casks are filled with sherry, used, and then sent to Orkney for use in the maturation process.

The distillery is owned by the Edrington Group who are also the producers of the renowned The Macallan.

Tour Details

For tour information, opening times and to book a tour please visit *https://www.highlandparkwhisky.com/en/visit*—Bookings must be made in advance. Guided Tours through a 18th Century malt whisky distiller that concludes with a wee dram.

Enjoy your visit

Tlachd as do chuairt

DISTILLERY 8
SCAPA DISTILLERY
ST. OLA, KIRKWALL, KW15 1SE

SCAPA DISTILLERY

01856 873269
scapa.admin@pernod-ricard.com
https://www.scapawhisky.com

Located on the A964, the distillery first opened in 1885. The Scapa

Distillery looks out onto Scapa Flow – a vast sheltered natural harbour. It uses water, which is heavily peated from Lingro Burn and a local spring.

Scapa is the Norse word for "to create" and the brand symbol is the Orkney Yole, a traditional seafaring Norse boat. The barley is unpeated and the single malts are exclusively aged in bourbon casks where the inside staves have been charred. Scapa has a floral, salty smooth taste. A team of only five operators man the distillery, producing Scapa Skiren. Owned by Chivas Brothers, part of Pernod–Ricard

Tour Details

Shop open Monday to Thursday 13.00 to 17.00.

Scapa Tours with tutored tastings with 2 drams are available at 10.00, 13.15 and 16.00 - *Monday to Saturday*. Sunday 13.15 and 16.00. Scapa Tour is £12 per person. Duration 45 minutes. Children over 8 permitted.

Lomond Tours available with 3 drams for £25 per person. *Monday to Saturday,* 11.00 and *Monday, Wednesday, Friday and Sunday* at 14.00. duration 90minutes.

Macfarlane & Townsend Tours are £40 per person with 7 tutored whisky samples. *Tuesday, Thursday and Saturday* at 14.00. Over 18s only. Duration 2 hours.

All tours must be pre – booked. Bookings can be made online. Complimentary bottles for whisky samples are available to drivers. Private Tastings 11.00 to 12.00 by appointment only.

Enjoy your visit

Tlachd as do chuairt

Overnight stop at Kirkwall

HIGHLAND PARK WHISKY SHOP
58 ALBERT STREET, KW15 1HQ
01856 885604

The most extensive range of Highland Park whiskies. Also includes a small art gallery for local artists. A must visit.

ORKNEY HOTEL
40 VICTORIA STREET, KW15 1DN
01856 873477

An extensive range of whiskies, including some from closed distilleries, can be found at this hotel that dates back to 1670. Five course whisky dinners are available.

THE FOVERAN, KW15 1SF (A964)
01856 872389

A family run restaurant specialising in shellfish and Orkney cuisine.

THE STOREHOUSE RESTAURANT WITH ROOMS, BRIDGE STREET WYND, KW15 1JD
01856 872389

A modern renovated restaurant situated in the centre of historic Kirkwall.

HARBOUR FRY, BRIDGE STREET KW15 1HR
01856 873170

Best fish and chips and location.

VISIT SCOTLAND I CENTRE, KIRKWALL

West Castle Street, KW15 1GU
01856 872856

CONSIDER TAKING A ROUND TRIP, USING BOTH FERRIES!

Distances cannot be calculated accurately as it will be dependent on the car ferry chosen.

Ferry crossing rates are correct as of March 2021.

DAY THREE KIRKWALL CENTRE

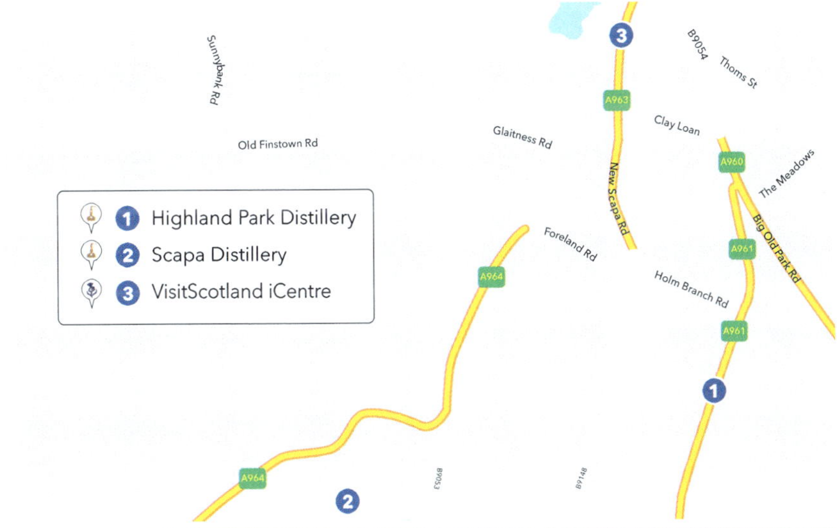

DAY FOUR MAP – KIRKWALL TO ULLAPOOL

SECTION 6

Day Four
Kirkwall, Orkney to Ullapool

WHERE WILL YOU DEPART FROM?

The departure location will be dependent on the car ferries you chose or if you had opted out and continued directly to Ullapool.

THURSO

The most northerly mainland town in the UK. Thurso is derived from an old Norse word *Thorso*—River of the God Thor.

LINDSAY GALLACHER STUDIO & WORKSHOP, 1–3 BRABSTER STREET, KW14 7AP
07779 232782

Make your own silver jewellery. If you have an interest in art, this is a wonderful shop and workshop where you can make, buy or view how silver jewellery is created.

Today is a drive of some 181 miles with no distillery visits.

Some 9 miles west of Thurso is the Dounreay Reactor, commissioned in 1955. You'll see the dome for several miles.

From	Kirkwall to Stromness car ferry
To	Scrabster
Road	A965
Miles	15
Time	21 minutes

THEN:

From	Scrabster
To	Durness
Road	A836 & A838
Miles	71
Time	1h 53m

TONGUE TO DURNESS, JOIN THE A838

This is a long stretch of coastal road traversing the most northerly coast of Scotland from East to West. The views are spectacular, and the weather can be changeable even on a summers' day.

Good stopping points are the villages of Bettyhill and Tongue some 31 and 44 miles respectively, from Thurso. After Bettyhill, watch out for the narrow bridge over the river Naver.

THE KYLE OF TONGUE

A shallow sea loch, traversed by a causeway and bridge.

BEN HOPE

The most northerly Munro (mountain), *Ben Hope* can be seen from the road. Additionally, *Ben Loyal* is also visible on the horizon.

SMOO CAVE, LEIRINMORE, IV27 4QA

Just before Durness, Smoo (Norse for a hiding place or hole) Cave has a car park and steep, stepped path to the entrance of the cave. There is a viewing platform for the waterfall.

BALNAKEIL BAY

Balnakeil beach

A wonderful, photographic stretch of sandy beach.

COCOA MOUNTAIN CHOCOLATIERS IV27 4PT

By the beach at Balnakeil Bay, this shop has received great acclaim for their hot chocolate.

JOHN LENNON MEMORIAL GARDENS DURNESS VILLAGE HALL, IV27 4QA

The Lennon-Onos

As a child, John Lennon visited here with his family from the age of nine. His family visited cousins while on many summer holidays. John returned in 1969 with Yoko Ono and their children, Julian and Kyoko.

From	**Durness**
To	**Skiag Bridge**
Road	**A838, A894 & A837**
Miles	**44**
Time	**1h 04m**

LAXFORD BRIDGE

Take care to follow the A894 to Ullapool at this junction.

KYLESKU BRIDGE & KYLESKU HOTEL IV27 4HW

Kylesku Bridge

The bridge has wonderful vistas of Loch Glendhu—Ove Arup, the consultants on the bridge, also worked on the the Sydney Opera House. The hotel is ideal for lunch or a coffee stop. (35 miles from Durness).

THERE IS THE NARROW ROAD (B869) THAT GOES FROM KYLESKU TO LOCHINVER (NOT RECOMMENDED)

If you do travel to Lochinver, it is best to take the A837 and then return back to the A837. A round trip of some 26 miles and 45 minutes.

From	Skiag Bridge
To	Lochinver and back
Road	A837
Miles	26
Time	36 minutes

This detour is optional. Consider the route timing before making the journey.

THE LOCHINVER LARDER MAIN STREET, IV27 4JY

01571 844356

Recommended for fans of pies! The Larder is world-renowned for its selection of local produce and sensational, sweet and savoury pies. A restaurant is also available.

ALBANNACH HOTEL & RESTAURANT BADDIDARROCH, IV27 4LP

01571 844537

Only 8 tables but holds a Michelin star (2009).

ON THE EDGE OF THE RIVER INVER AND LOCHINVER

Stunning sea views.

Return to Skaig Bridge.

From	Skiag Bridge
To	Ledmore
Road	A837
Miles	7
Time	9 minutes

LEDMORE

At the junction, take the A835 to Ullapool.

The Highland Coast (HC 700) Whisky Route

From	Ledmore
To	Ullapool
Road	A835
Miles	18
Time	26 minutes

Daily Total	181 Miles	4h 29m

Overnight stop at Ullapool

Ullapool

Ullapool is on the shores of Loch Broom. The car ferry departs here for Stornoway (Lewis and Harris). Great fresh seafood is landed at the harbour. Boat trips available to the Summer Isles but are seasonal. A wide range of accommodation is available, however it is extremely busy in the summer season, so book well in advance.

ROYAL HOTEL (INC. THE WHISKY GANTRY), GARVE ROAD, IV26 2SY
01854 612181

The restaurant has a fine selection of traditional Scottish dishes along with a wonderful array of seafood, local fish and Italian cuisine.The bar has a wide range of 300 whiskies with a great atmosphere and extremely knowledgable staff. All you need to know about the best malt whiskies. The bar also serves food to accompany your chosen malt. Great views of the Loch Broom.

ULLAPOOL SMOKEHOUSE
UNIT 6A MOREFIELD IND. ESTATE
IV26 2SR
01854 613881

Superb malt whisky smoked salmon. Also available is heather-infused smoked salmon. Delightful and a definite must-visit.

THE CEILIDH PLACE
14 WEST ARGYLE STREET, IV26 2TY
01854 612103

Live music, art gallery, restaurant and bookshop all in one location. Quirky, and a must see.

HIGHLAND LIQUOR COMPANY BOTTLE SHOP
26 WEST ARGYLE STREET, IV26 2TY

THE SEAFOOD SHACK
WEST ARGYLE STREET
IV26 2TY
07876 142623

Only open in the summer months, here you'll find great fresh seafood, bang on season. Outdoor seating area with takeaway. You can also buy the fresh product if you are in self-catering accommodation. Try the 'Spinys' (small squat lobsters only found in the West Coast of Scotland) with hot butter and garlic or the Mayo Langoustines. The fish and shellfish come straight off the small fishing boats in the harbour. Do not forget to buy your personally signed cookbook!

THE SEAFORTH
QUAY STREET, IV26 2UE
01854 612122

Excellent fish and chips takeaway and location.

VISIT SCOTLAND I CENTRE, ULLAPOOL

Argyle Street, IV26 2UB
01854 612486

Hand-dived scallops, langoustines, crab, mussels, prawns and many varieties of fresh fish are available in Ullapool as they are in many other towns and villages along the HC 700.

Gorse

The Highland Coast (HC 700) Whisky Route

DAY FIVE OVERVIEW

SECTION 7

Day Five
Ullapool to the Isle of Skye

A MEMORABLE JOURNEY

From	Ullapool
To	Gairloch
Road	A835 & A832
Miles	57
Time	1h 19m

BRAEMORE

Just after this small village take the A832 road to Gairloch.

INVEREWE GARDEN, IV22 2LG

A botanical oasis founded in 1862 with over 2,500 exotic flowers and plants. Museum and café. National Trust for Scotland heritage garden where the effects of the Gulf Stream create a microclimate ideal for plants to thrive.

LOCHEWE

A small village by Loch Ewe. The River Ewe is one of the shortest in Scotland.

From	Gairloch
To	Kinlochewe
Road	A832
Miles	21
Time	29 minutes

GAIRLOCH

A quaint village close to Loch Maree. Sea trips available and a visit to the stately Victorian era Gairloch Hotel recommended.

KINLOCHEWE

Turn right onto the A896 to Sheildaig.

From	Kinlochewe
To	Sheildaig
Road	A896
Miles	18
Time	29 minutes

The Highland Coast (HC 700) Whisky Route

BICELLUM BRASIERI

A billion-year-old fossil found in the Highlands could be the earliest multicellular animal recorded by science so far.

The microscopic fossil was discovered at Loch Torridon in Wester Ross by researchers led by the University of Sheffield and the US's Boston College. Researchers say the earliest forms of life on Earth may have developed in freshwater, rather than the ocean.

THE TORRIDON HOTEL
BY ACHNASHEEN, WESTER ROSS
IV22 2EY
01445 791242

Torradon Hotel

A grand, turreted 5-star hotel offering an acclaimed whisky bar and restaurant. Recently featured on ITVs This Morning with John Torrode.

THE TORRIDON HOTEL WHISKY BAR
01445 791242

Stocked with 365 single malt whiskies (and 120 gins), one whisky for every day of the year! This bar was once named the Best Whisky Bar in the World by Whisky Magazine. Book a whisky tasting experience. The hotel rears its own Highland beef and pork within the farm and kitchen garden in the hotel grounds.

A896

This road runs alongside beautiful Upper Loch Torridon.

SHEILDAIG

A small, picturesque fishing village.

At Sheildaig, there is a small road that goes to Applecross. This road is part of the NC 500 Route. We do not recommend this route unless you are an adventurous and competent driver. There are many passing places but in the summer months, this part of the NC 500 receives numerous complaints about the chaos of the traffic. In early spring, late autumn and the winter months it can be extremely difficult. There are many other wonderful views on the HC 700.

From	**Sheildaig**
To	**Strathcarron**
Road	**A896**
Miles	**20**
Time	**33 minutes**

KISHORN SEAFOOD BAR
IV54 8XA
01520 733240

Located at the head of Loch Kishorn, this is a real seafood-lovers haven, with stunning views towards Skye and the Cuillin Hills. Features daily catches from local boats. Try the squat lobster. Slightly difficult to find the seafood bar, but ask for directions.

STRATHCARRON

Take the right turn onto the A890.

From	**Strathcarron**
To	**Kyle of Lochalsh**
Road	**A890 & A87**
Miles	**20**
Time	**27 minutes**

LOCH CARRON

Drive along the shores of this picturesque loch.

A87, KIRKTON

Just after Kirkton, right turn onto the A87, then cross the Skye Bridge to the Isle of Skye.

From	**Kyle of Lochalsh**
To	**Harriport**
Road	**A87**
Miles	**8**
Time	**12 minutes**

SKYE BRIDGE

Skye Bridge

A visit to the Isle of Skye (the Misty Isle) will be a memorable journey. Skye lies in the Inner Hebrides and is home to the Black Cuillin Mountains with many narrow mountain lochs and dramatic coastal scenery. Whisky distilled in Skye is from the Highland Region, but many experts say the Islands should have their own regional whisky category.

The two Skye distilleries are in different directions, so it may be best to choose in advance what your personal whisky itinerary will be.

If you choose to visit Talisker only, then the best island route is to travel directly to Carbost on the A87, and then onwards staying overnight in Portree.

If you decide to visit both distilleries, then it is perhaps best to visit the Torabhaig Distillery first.

THE MISTY BOTTLE
OLD POST OFFICE, BREAKISH
IV42 8PY
01471 820348

Just after this quaint whisky and gift shop and before Harrapool, turn right off the A87 and onto the A851.

From	**Harrapool**
To	**Teangue**
Road	**A851**
Miles	**11**
Time	**14 minutes**

From	**Teangue**
To	**Harrapool**
Road	**A851**
Miles	**11**
Time	**14 minutes**

DISTILLERY 9
TORABHAIG DISTILLERY
TEANGUE, SKYE, IV44 8RE

TORABHAIG DISTILLERY

01471 833447
info@torabhaig.com
https://www.torabhaig.com

THE DISTILLERY AT
TORABHAIG
ISLE OF SKYE

The distillery at Torabhaig is truly a product of its surroundings and heritage, shaped by the wild landscape and climate of the Isle of Skye. We first found it as an abandoned but ruggedly handsome farm steading which just so happened to be the perfect location for a distillery. In February 2021 we released our first Single Malt Scotch Whisky, Torabhaig 2017—The Legacy Series.

Tour Details

Our visitor experience includes tours of the distillery, a whisky shop and café serving light lunches, refreshments and home baking. The farm steading is built around a courtyard where visitors can enjoy their refreshments when the weather is clement. The tour is around 45 minutes–1 hour long and costs £10. Our opening times can vary so please check the 'Distillery Tours' page on our website—*torabhaig.com*—for current opening times and where you will also be able to book your tour.

Enjoy your visit

Tlachd as do chuairt

After the distillery visit, head back to the A87, continuing on to Carbost.

From	**Harrapool**
To	**Carbost**
Road	**A87, A863 & B8009**
Miles	**25**
Time	**33 minutes**

SLIGACHAN

This is a good viewpoint for the Black Cuillin Mountains. Turn off the A87 onto the A863.

Turn left off the A863 onto the smaller road B8009 to the Talisker Distillery.

DISTILLERY 10
TALISKER DISTILLERY
CARBOST, IV47 8SR

TALISKER DISTILLERY

01478 614308
malts@intervino.co.uk
https://www.malts.com/en-row/distilleries/talisker

Dramatic views of the magnificent Cuillin Hills from the distillery. The water descends from Hawk Hill, it is very peaty and can appear a reddish colour, due to the influence of the peat bog.

Hints of strong peppery smoke from the water and the peat. With the background maritime notes from a coastal distillery. Talisker recommends fresh oysters with their whisky, for the ultimate sensory experience. Operating since 1831. Talisker single malt became one of the largest selling single malt whiskies by the turn of the 20th century. Such was the demand for Talisker whisky, that the distillery had a pier and small tramway built. The distillery is owned by Diageo.

Tour Details

Flavours of Talisker – An introduction to Talisker whisky including three drams. This experience operates every day on an hourly basis. 45 minute tour costing £15.

Talisker Cask Tasting - Tutored tasting with four unique drams, only one tour per day at 13.30. 45 minute tour costing £25.

Open every day. Advance bookings essential. Visitor Centre and shop.

Enjoy your visit

Tlachd as do chuairt

OPTIONAL TRIP

DUNVEGAN CASTLE & GARDENS
IV55 8WF
01470 521206

Ancestral home of the Clan Macleod and the oldest continuously inhabited castle in Scotland. Tours of the castle and gardens are available. Restaurant and café available. 21 miles from Carbost on the A863.

Please allow extra time if you wish to visit Dunvegan Castle.

From	Carbost
To	Portree
Road	B8009, A863 & A87
Miles	17
Time	24 minutes

Daily Total	208 Miles	5h 34m

Overnight stop at Portree

PORTREE

Very pretty harbour scene with houses painted in delightful pastel colours.

HARBOUR CHIP SHOP
1 QUAY STREET, PORTREE
IV51 9DE

Great fish & chips in this picturesque harbour.

THE VIEW RESTAURANT
CUILLIN HILLS HOTEL
SCORRYBREAC ROAD
PORTREE, IV51 9QU
01478 612003

Situated in front of fabulous views looking towards the Cuillin Hills, and looking down on Portree harbour.

Portree Harbour

Local Scottish produce with a large selection of seafood.

THE MALT WHISKY EMBASSY
CUILLIN HILLS HOTEL
IV51 9QU

Over 130 malt whiskies available. Sophisticated and relaxing whisky bar with knowledgeable staff.

SCORRYBREAC RESTAURANT
7 BOSVILLE TERRACE
PORTREE, IV51 9DG
01478 612069

Local produce from the Misty Isle with thoughtful seasonal cuisine.

THE GRANARY
SOMERLED SQUARE
PORTREE, IV51 9EH
01478 612873

A relaxed café in the main sqaure of Portree, offering a great range of breads and pastries as well as excellent coffee—sit outside and watch life go by...

VISIT SCOTLAND I CENTRE, PORTREE

Bayfield Road, Portree, IV26 2UB
01478 612992

Notes

The Highland Coast (HC 700) Whisky Route

DAY SIX – ISLE OF SKYE TO INVERNESS

SECTION 8

Day Six
Isle of Skye to Inverness

THE FINAL LEG!

This final drive involves departing from Skye on A87 before heading east to Invermoriston, following the road to Drumnadrochit and passing through part of the Great Glen. This drive travels along the shores of Loch Ness to Inverness via the Glen Ord Distillery in Muir of Ord.

From	Portree
To	Invermoriston
Road	A87 & A887
Miles	86
Time	1h 53m

SHIEL BRIDGE

If you wish to visit Eilean Donan Castle you will see the signs some 11 miles from the Skye Bridge.

EILEAN DONAN CASTLE
DORNIE, BY KYLE OF LOCHALSH
IV40 8DX
01599 555781 (CASTLE CAFÉ)

A small island that features this most iconic 13th Century Castle. Probably one of Scotland's most photographed site. Bookings are recommended.

BUN LOYNE

At Bun Loyne, take the A887 to Invermoriston.

From	Invermoriston
To	Drumnadrochit
Road	A82
Miles	14
Time	21 minutes

A82

Drive along the shores of legendary Loch Ness. Loch Ness has one of the RNLI inland rescue stations: *Temple Pier, IV63 6XR.* Loch Ness has more fresh water than all the lakes in England. Peat particles from the hills means the loch is almost dark at the deepest parts.

URQUHART CASTLE, IV63 6XJ

Iconic and picturesque, the ruined castle overlooks Loch Ness.

Urquhart Castle, Great Glen

GREAT GLEN

Also known as Glen Albyn or Glen More, this glen runs for 62 miles from Inverness to Fort William. It follows a geological fault line that bisects the Scottish Highlands. It was created some 400 million years ago. A large portion of the glen is filled with 5 mainly fresh-water lochs including Loch Ness. Loch Linnhe on the western side of the Glen is a sea loch which flows out to the Firth of Lorne and into the Irish Sea.

DRUMNADROCHIT

A village on the western shore of Loch Ness, home to the legendary Loch Ness monster!

FIDDLERS BAR & HIGHLAND RESTAURANT

THE VILLAGE GREEN
DRUMNADROCHIT (LOCH NESS)
IV63 6TX
01456 450678

An award-wining venue, famous for its salmon, beef, haggis and game dishes. It also has the ever popular *Top Ten Desert Island Drams*. The bar offers 'whisky flights' so a range of whiskies can be tasted. Music on certain nights.

LOCH NESS CENTRE & NESSIE EXHIBITION

IV63 6TU
01456 450573

Tourist attraction focusing on the local 'Nessie monster!'. Museum, gift shop, whisky shop and kiltmakers. The first recorded sighting of the world-famous Loch Ness Monster or 'Nessie' was by St Columba 565 AD whilst on his way to convert the Pictish King Brude.

CLANSMAN HOTEL & VISITOR CENTRE
IV63 8AU
01456 450326

Lochside location with boat pier for Loch Ness Cruises, a great whiskey, gift shop and restaurant overlooking the Loch. Best gift shop in the highlands!

CALEDONIAN CANAL

Built by Thomas Telford and completed in 1822, the canal connects the lochs in the Great Glen from Inverness to Fort William and provides a ship route that avoids the hazardous Pentland Firth. Maximum boat length is 150 feet and 35 feet width. There are 29 locks and 10 swing bridges.

From	Drumnadrochit
To	Muir of Ord
Road	A831, A833, A862 & A832
Miles	16
Time	25 minutes

MILTON

About one mile out of Drumnadrochit take the right turn onto the A833.

AFTER KILTARLITY

Take the A862 to Muir of Ord..

MUIR OF ORD

The Glen Ord Distillery is on the A832 on the outskirts of the village of Muir of Ord. You will see the sign for the Glen Ord Distillery.

DISTILLERY 11
GLEN ORD DISTILLERY
MUIR OF ORD, IV6 7UI

GLEN ORD DISTILLERY

01463 872004
glen.ord@malts.com
https://www.malts.com/en-row/distilleries/the-singleton-of-glen-ord

Founded in 1838, this distillery produces The Singleton of Glen Ord malt whisky. There are 2 other Singleton whiskies which are distilled in the Speyside region and they are exported to Europe and the US. The current distillery is allegedly close to the demolished Ferintosh distillery and mentioned in the History of Whisky. Peat is taken from local mossy banks, cut in the Spring and then taken to the distillery in August for storage. Glen Ord produces and supplies peat and malted barley to many other distilleries such as Talisker on the isle of Skye. The Singleton of Glen Ord is a sweet rich whisky - the flavour profile includes toffee, dried fruit and vanilla among others. The Singleton of Glen Ord is mostly exported to South East Asia. The majority of its' whisky is sold as a 12 year old single malt at 40% ABV. The 12year old is currently the number one whisky in Singapore. The distillery is owned by Diageo.

Tour Details

Singleton of Glen Ord Tasting Experience—£5 for a tutored tasting.
Signature Experience—£10 with a guided distillery tour and tasting.
Visitor Centre & Whisky Shop. A Virtual Tour is available to view online.

Enjoy your visit

Tlachd as do chuairt

From	**Muir of Ord**
To	**Beauly**
Road	**A832, A862**
Miles	**5**
Time	**5m**

From	**Beauly**
To	**Inverness**
Road	**A862**
Miles	**14**
Time	**24m**

BEAULY FIRTH

Here the road travels along the southern side of the Firth.

DOWNRIGHT GABBLER
HIGH STREET, BEAULY, IV4 7BT
01463 782800

Here at the Downright Gabbler they offer you the chance to explore Highland history and culture, in a fun way, using the best of Scottish food and drink. Unique, delicious and entertaining. A must try!

Daily Total	**135 Miles**	**3h 48m**
Total Miles: 700		

Notes

CONGRATULATIONS

(meala-naid beachd)

ON COMPLETING THE HIGHLAND COAST 700 WHISKY ROUTE!

If you have a HC 700 Whisky Passport, please forward this to Spirit of the Glen Ltd. and your Certificate will be issued.

Your Whisky Route passport can either be emailed or posted. Full contact details on the passport.

SECTION 9

Top 10 Planning Tips for the HC 700 Whisky Route

1. *Maps* – Ordinance Survey (OS) Road Map 1 A great asset on the trip. You will also need a good map of Skye. Consider downloading the App that converts OS grid references to postal codes. *gridreferencefinder.com*

2. *List of Recommended Equipment* – Warm, waterproof clothing, boots, hat, umbrella, torch, disposable travel poncho, small backpack, bottles of water, light snacks, binoculars, sunglasses, insect spray, high vis over-jacket. An extra pair of dry socks could be useful and welcome!

3. *Weather and Hours of Daylight* – Hours of daylight in the Highlands vary enormously between summer and winter. Summer daylight can start at 04.30 to 22.30. Winter daylight can reduce to 08.30 to 15.30.

4. *WiFi, Mobile Networks and Cameras* – Signal strength can be poor or non-existent in certain northern and western areas, so Sat. Nav. is invaluable. If you have a modern mobile phone with superb pixel quality, then you will be assured great photos and communications. However, as the scenery is spectacular, large number of tourists use SLR cameras. A SLR camera could be a useful purchase on this trip. It is your choice - they both have their merits.

5 *Planning and Local Information* – Planning is a vital ingredient for a successful trip such as the HC 700 Whisky Route. Do spend time considering your trip and personal objectives. If you are in doubt, or are lost, or just need help during your travels on the Whisky Route - ask a local. They will generally be happy to assist. Always locate and use the Visit Scotland i Centre tourist offices. Location and contact details are shown in the daily travel schedule.

6. *Local Highland Cuisine* – Do be adventurous and try local dishes.

You will be pleasantly surprised. A sample list of Highland Cuisine is shown in Section 16.

7. *Insects and Repellent* – The most ferocious local pest is the 'midgie' (Culicoidas inpunctatus). The female is the 'bloodthirsty' one! Midges do not differentiate between animals and humans, so ensure you take relevant products with you including anti-sting gel, cream or spray. Antihistamine tablets or cream might be wise if your skin is sensitive. Midge head/ face nets are available on Amazon; if the clouds of midges are bad, you will be glad you came prepared. The only other nuisance, but very rarely seen, is the adder. The only venomous snake in the UK, but generally the bite is painful but not deadly. Recognisable by the zig zag pattern on its' skin. Very elusive and will only infrequently be seen sunning on rocks.

8. *Night-Time Driving* – Try to avoid driving at night. Highland roads can be potentially dangerous to tourists unaware of local road conditions.

9. *Fuel* – Try to keep your car's fuel tank half full as a minimum. Fuel stations can be far apart on the North West Coast roads.

10. *Accommodation* – There is a great deal of accommodation on the HC 700 Whisky Route. Websites such as Booking.com, Air B&B, Trip Advisor, Visit Scotland i Centres and many other websites. All have a great deal of information on different types of accommodation that will best suit your budget.

Wild camping is less restricted than in England but increasingly, many wild camping sites are being closed. Authorised camp sites are plentiful. It is important to plan and book accommodation in advance. In the summer months, there can be an acute shortage of accommodation.

SECTION 10

Other Whisky & Spirit Distilleries, Whisky Cocktails and Scottish Slang

There are more than 130 active whisky distilleries in Scotland. These are located in the five most recognised whisky distilling regions.

Other whisky distilleries on the HC 700 Whisky Route:

TOULVADDIE DISTILLERY
FEARN AERODROME, FEARN
TARN IV20 1XW

01862 808138
info@toulvaddie.co.uk
https://www.toulvaddiedistillery.com

Built on the site of a former Royal Navy airbase (HMS Owl), north of Inverness and just a stones' throw from the well- established Glenmorangie Distillery, Toulvaddie is a brand new micro distillery and the first Scotch whisky distillery to be founded solely by a woman in over 200 years. Initially, production will be 30,000 litres per year, with a limited number of Year One casks available to purchase. It is also possible to join the Toulvaddie Founders Members Club.

Still under construction but advance purchase of cask whisky available.

Not open to the public

TEANINICH DISTILLERY
RIVERSIDE DRIVE
ALNESS, IV17 0XB

01349 885001

The most recognised product is the Flora and Fauna 10 year old Single Malt.

The distillery is owned by Diageo.

Not open to the public

INVERGORDON DISTILLERY
GOLFVIEW TERRACE
IV18 0HP

01349 852451

A high volume grain only distillery.

Not open to the public

THOMPSON BROS DISTILLERY
DORNOCH CASTLE HOTEL
CASTLE STREET
DORNOCH IV25 3SD

01862 810637
info@dornochdistillery.com
https://www.thompsonbrosdistillery.com

Set up in the quirky old 'Fire House' in the grounds of Dornoch Castle Hotel, this micro distillery started producing gin in December 2016 and laid its first whisky cask down in January 2017.

Not open to the public

WOLFBURN DISTILLERY
HENDERSON PARK, THURSO,
CAITHNESS, KW14 7XW

01847 891051
info@wolfburn.com
https://www.wolfburn.com

Wolfburn began producing whisky in January 2013, making it one of Scotland's newest distilleries. The new distillery is actually a reincarnation of the old Wolfburn Distillery (founded in 1821) and draws its water from the same burn as the original distillery. Wolfburn whisky was first launched in 2016. Owned by a Private Consortium.

Visits are possible; there is a shop but no visitor centre

BADACHRO DISTILLERY
AIRD HILL, BADACHRO
GAIRLOCH, IV21 2AB

01445 741282
gordon@badachrodistillery.com
https://www.badachrodistillery.com

A small family managed distillery producing small batch artisan whisky and gin.

Very friendly tour and shop

ISLE OF SKYE DISTILLERS
PORTREE, IV51 9EJ

01478 611117

Misty Isle is the gin here. A modern shop with a small distillery attached. Skye enterprise at its best. It also has a Gin School. Try the raspberry pink gin.

GLENWYVIS DISTILLERY
1 UPPER DOCHCARTY
DINGWALL, IV15 9UF

01349 862005
info@glenwvyis.com
https://www.glenwvyis.com

Nestled beneath the sprawling mass of Ben Wyvis mountain is the GlenWyvis Distillery which was established in 2015. The idea was to unite the community of Dingwall through the creation of a distillery owned in part by local people.

More than 3000 like-minded people invested in GlenWyvis to create the first ever 100% community owned distillery. The first whisky goes on sale in 2021.

Casks available for purchase.

Virtual tours only

GIN DISTILLERIES

Not everybody drinks Scotch but Scotland and the Highlands do have other spirits to offer. The clear liquid that emerges from the early whisky distilling process can be readily converted to gin with the addition of botanicals such as juniper berries, coriander, angelica root, cinnamon, orris root, cassis bark, licorice, lemon and orange zest—some even add cucumber.

Scotland produces many of the more famous high street gin brands. Perhaps surprisingly, some 65% of the UKs gin is produced in Scotland.

Unusually, London Gin does not have to be distilled in London, but it must have the majority of its botanical as juniper berries.

DORNOCH DISTILLERY
(THOMPSON BROS)
CASTLE CLOSE, IV25 3SD

01349 862005

The distillery produces gin, and is based in the grounds of Dornoch Castle Hotel. Whisky has been laid down, but is not yet available for sale.

DUNNET HEAD DISTILLERY
DUNNET, CAIHNESS
KW14 8XD

01847 851287

Located at Dunnet Head, this distillery produces Rock Rose Gin. For gin drinkers on the Whisky Route, a visit to this gin distillery is a most enjoyable and educational experience.

LOCH NESS SPIRITS
DORES, LOCH NESS
IV2 6TU

01847 851287

Although not technically on the HC 700, this is a small batch gin distillery. Dores is located on the southern side of Loch Ness, some nine miles from Inverness on the B862. Visits are by appointment only. The family have lived on the shores of Loch Ness for five centuries. A very personal experience.

NORTH POINT DISTILLERY
THURSO, KW14 7UZ

01847 808120

The distillery uses the finest sugar cane and molasses from the Caribbean to distill its rum. The rum is matured in whisky casks.

SUGGESTED WHISKY COCKTAILS

THE AFFINITY

Scotch whisky Manhattan. Scotch with equal amounts of sweet and dry vermouth and orange bitters.

ROB ROY

Scotch, sweet vermouth and bitters.

RUSTY NAIL

Scotch and Drambuie.

GODFATHER

Scotch and Amaretto.

The Highland Coast (HC 700) Whisky Route

Whisky flights

GOLD MINE

Scotch, sherry, Galliano, lime juice, lemonade and egg white.

BLOOD AND SAND

Scotch, sweet vermouth, cherry brandy and orange juice.

SCOTCH SOUR

Scotch on ice with lemon juice.

SCOTCH AND SODA

A simple cocktail. Add soda to your preference.

ROBERT BURNS

Add orange bitters and absinthe to a Rob Roy.

MAMIE TAYLOR

Scotch with ginger beer and a hint of lime.

TODDY

Whisky, honey, lemon with hot water added. Can also be drunk cold. Heather honey is best. Ideal hot drink for a chilly night or relieving the symptoms of a cold or flu.

GILLY FIX

Scotch with peach brandy, rum, lemon juice and a simple sugar over crushed ice.

ANGEL'S SHARE

Only for the immortal!

THE BEST WAY

Scotch with a little water and no ice! Absolutely applicable to a malt whisky.

SOME SCOTTISH WORDS

Alba *n.* Scotland

Beastie *adj.* Familiar and affectionate term for a small animal or insect

Bonnie *adj.* pretty, attractive, beautiful; can be applied to females or males

Braw *adj.* *Also* bra' or braa. Of things; fine, splendid, illustrious

Burn *n.* A brook or stream, also known as the water used in brewing

Clipe *vb.* Also clype, klipe, claip. To tell tales about or inform against someone

Dreich *adj.* Long-drawn-out, protracted, hence tedious, wearisome, damp, rainy weather

Glaikit *adj.* Also gleckit, gleekit. Stupid, foolish, thoughtless, irresponsible, flighty

Gloamin *n.* Evening, twilight, dusk

Haver *vb.* Also haiver. To talk in a foolish or trivial manner, speak nonsense, to babble, gossip

Ken *vb.* To know, be aware of, apprehend, learn

Neeps *n.* Turnip, often served with haggis and tatties

Nyaff *n.* Also nyaf. A small, conceited, impudent, chattering fellow

Piece *n.* A piece of bread and butter, jam, or the like, a snack, usually of bread, scone or oatcake, a sandwich

Scunnered *vb.* Also scunnert. To make (one) bored, uninterested or antipathetic

Shoogle *vb.* Also shoggle, schochle. To shake, joggle, to cause to totter or rock, to swing backwards and forwards

Sleekit *adj.* Insinuating, sly, cunning, specious, not altogether to be trusted

Stappit *adj.* Blocked, choked, stuffed or stop

Totie *n.* Also totty, toatie. Small, diminutive, tiny

Wheest *vb.* Also whisht, weesht. To silence, to cause to be quiet, to hush, quieten

SECTION 11

The History of Scotch Whisky (Uisge Beatha), Scotland and the Whisky Regions

A LONG AND ILLUSTRIOUS HISTORY...

Scotch whisky was first recorded in the Exchequer Rolls of Scotland in 1494. Friar John Cor, a monk based at Lindores Abbey, Newbury, Fife was the distiller.

Whisky was an essential part of Gaelic life and history. Recorded as a medicinal remedy for a cold or fever (with added honey), or simply to keep the Highland cold weather at bay or indeed, as an anaesthetic for sword wounds, operations or childbirth. Primarily, it was for hospitality and social gatherings like Ceilidhs for which the Highlanders were renowned throughout the world.

Written in James IVs Treasury Accounts in 1506, was a request for *Aqua Vitae (Uisge Beatha or Water of Life)* during a visit to Inverness.

Inverness is also the start and finish of the HC 700 Whisky Route some 500 years later!

1690 was the earliest reference to a distillery; this was the *Ferintosh* Distillery, owned by Duncan Fraser of Culloden, and recorded in the Acts of Scottish Parliament†.

In 1660, Excise Tax was introduced on alcohol. In the Highlands, many illicit stills continued to operate without paying excise tax.

In 1771, Edinburgh had eight licenced distilleries and an estimated 400 illegal stills. The Scots never really approved of paying Excise Custom Duty on whisky. Please read the notes at the bottom of this Section to see how much Custom Duty and VAT we are paying today. You will be surprised!

In 1781, it became illegal to privately distil whisky. Many *"boot-leggers"* grew into some of today's major brands such as Lagavulin and Bowmore and many others. Highland Park and Glenlivet can also trace their roots to

Illicit stills

†*see Burns poem about Ferintosh on page 77*

bootlegging before distilleries were officially licenced.

In 1823 the Excise Act (Duty) was passed. It ended the massive smuggling and illicit stills that were common in Scotland.

Scotch whisky had an unusual and fortuitous opportunity in the 1870s when Cognac vanished due to the Phylloxera crisis. This small insect destroyed great swathes of French vineyards. Scotch stepped into the vacuum this created and became the spirit of choice in the world. It rapidly gained an international following.

Old Distillery Workers

Scotch is still the spirit of choice in many countries around the world.

World Whisky Day is the 3rd Saturday of May

The three oldest working distilleries in Scotland are:

1. *GLENTURRET 1775, Crieff, Perthshire.*

2. *BOWMORE 1779, Isle of Islay.*

3. *STRATHISLA 1786, Keith, Banffshire.*

All are operating today on their original site.

Scotch has evolved superbly since those earlier times and is now surely the world's greatest spirit. It is certainly Scotland's most celebrated export.

STYLES OF SCOTCH WHISKY

Malt Whisky

Malt whisky can only be made with malted barley. No other grains can be used. A single malt can either be from a single distillery or a single barrel. Malts can also be vatted (mixed). Malts are more complex than blends and can vary significantly within the same distillery. Factors such as the distilling process, the water source, the type of oak barrel, age or the maturation period have an impact. Rarely are two malts the same in aroma and taste profile.

Blended Whisky
Blends can use a range of alternative grains. The more expensive blended whiskies tend to have more malt scotch in the blend. Blended whiskies can come from many distilleries. The art of blending is the most critical skill component and branded whiskies will use blending, to achieve a consistent flavour and taste.

Grain Whisky
Some Scotch whiskies only use 100% grain such as wheat. Generally, they are cheaper due to the column stills and continuous process. They also can have a slightly smoother taste.

Peat
Peat bogs abound in the Highlands and historically peat was used as a household fuel. Some whisky tends to be lighter in colour whilst others tend to be darker and peaty. The peat smokiness can be introduced via the water which flows through a peat bog or when the barley is malted using peat fumes from the malting floor. Lightly or deeply peated whisky is a personal preference.

Age
Scotch whisky must be a minimum of three years before it can be sold to the public. Some distilleries show the age of the whisky on the bottle. The age statement must be determined by the youngest aged whisky in the bottle. Typically, the older the whisky the more expensive it is.

Ingredients
Scotch whisky generally contains three simple ingredients: grain, Scottish water and yeast. The complexity of whisky lies in those three magical ingredients. Some whiskies may add flavouring to obtain a deeper colour. Caramel is sometimes used.

Whisky Stills
Generally there are two types of still:

A pot still is regarded as superior and generally made of copper. Copper acts as a catalyst and aids the purification of the distillate. Most pot still production is generally double distilled. The whisky can reach up to 70 per cent by volume. Great debate surrounds the perceived benefits from the different shapes used at the top of the still.

A column or continuous still is generally more complex and is made of stainless steel. Distillate is generally stronger and smoother in texture. However, a certain amount of flavour can be lost. These stills can also be called patent or Coffey stills. Coffey, an Irishman had the original idea and Stein a Scotsman developed the continuous process.

Scotch Whisky Producing Regions

It is generally regarded there are five main whisky producing regions in Scotland. These are the Highlands, Speyside, Lowlands, Campbeltown and Islay. Although some experts are now saying that the Islands are a distinct and separate region and that whisky from here should not be included in the Highland category.

The Highland Region. This Region has some 47 distilleries. It is the largest and most diverse area and includes the Scottish islands. An imaginary line drawn between the Firth of Tay and the Firth of Clyde would be the approximate boundary, so all distilleries north of this line will be classified as Highland. South of this line, the distilleries are regarded as Lowland whiskies. Many Highland distilleries whiskies have salty, maritime, coastal flavours that are so distinctly recognisable. This is certainly the case with whiskies distilled on Skye, Orkney, Jura, Mull, Arran and the Outer Hebrides. Highland whiskies have a scotch for all tastes and preferences. They are generally light and fragrant, except where peat is used. Some say they even have an unique taste from the heather.

The Speyside Region sits inside the Highland region but has its own distinct whiskies that are associated with the River Spey. This region has the highest concentration of distilleries. There is limited peat production here. The Speyside whiskies are more associated with hints of fruits like apple and pear, combined with vanilla and mild spice. Sherry casks are commonly used for the maturing process. Elegant and complex are terms often used in praise of a Speyside malt.

The Lowland Region is more famous for whiskies that have hints of toffee, toast or cinnamon. A lighter, smooth whisky, particularly with its malts.

The Islay Region (pronounced *eye-luh*) is a special category on its own. Famous for the pungent, heavily peaty, smoky and earthy characteristics of its unique whiskies. Medicinal is yet another term used to describe these Islay whiskies. It is the 'Magical Isle', where most islanders are involved in whisky production.

The Campbeltown Region. Distilling is much reduced with only three distilleries. It is also the smallest whisky region. Historically, it was regarded as the 'Whisky Capital of the World' with more than 30 distilleries. Today, the whiskies are varied and full of flavour. Sea salt, smoke, fruit, vanilla and toffee all mingle to create fine whiskies.

Casks

Scotch whisky, by law, must be stored in oak casks for a minimum of three years. The casks used are generally either American ex-bourbon or Spanish ex-sherry. American law requires that bourbon casks are used only once. Some casks are used more than once with Scotch whisky and that additional use can have a diminishing effect of flavour.

Quarter Cask—45 to 50 litre capacity.

Barrel—190 to 200 litre capacity.

Hogshead—225 to 250 litre capacity.

Whisky in a Cask

Barrique—250 to 300 litre capacity.

Puncheon—450 to 500 litre capacity.

Butt—475 to 500 litre capacity.

Port Pipes—550 to 650 litre capacity. Generally used to mature or 'finish' whisky in port casks.

Madeira Drum—600 to 650 litre capacity. Generally used to mature or 'finish' aged stocks of whisky in Madeira drums.

Casks can be *'first fill'* or *'refill'*. First fill are more active in the maturation process.

Alcohol Strength

Scotch whisky must be a minimum of 40% alcohol *(ABV)*. Many whiskies are sold at cask strength which is higher than 40% ABV.

Whisky or Whiskey?

Scotland and Canada use the spelling 'whisky', whereas in the USA and Ireland the spelling 'whiskey' applies.

The Scotch Whisky Sector generates approximately £5 billion for the UK economy. France is the largest export market for bottles, followed by India with the USA as the third by volume and higher value.

A Brief History of Scotland

1 Billion BC	Bicellum Brasieri emerge in Loch Torridon
390M BC	Great Glen created
4500 BC	Neolithic people recorded in Scotland
43 AD	Romans invade Britain
410	Romans depart from Britain
563	St. Columba founds the monastery on the Island of Iona
795	Viking raids on Scotland
1040	Macbeth crowned King of Scotland
1314	Robert Bruce fights at the Battle of Bannockburn
1587	Mary Queen of Scots is executed
1603	James VI becomes James I of England and consolidates the Stuart monarchy
1707	The Act of Union unites Scotland and England
1746	Bonnie Prince Charlie Stuart is defeated at Culloden
1759	Robert Burns Date of Birth 25th January (Burn's Night)
1762	Start of the Scottish Highland Clearances
1876	First telephone invented by Alexander Graham Bell
1881	Birth of Sir Alexander Fleming, discoverer of Penicillin
1890	Forth Rail Bridge opened
1901	Glenfinnan Viaduct opened Iconic scene of the Harry Potter Hogwarts Express
1930	Birth of Sir Sean Connery (Big Tam), born Thomas Connery
1965	Construction starts on the Queen Elizabeth 2 (QE 2) cruise ship. Built in the John Brown shipyards, Glasgow. Now moored in Dubai as a tourist attraction
1967	Drilling starts in the North Sea
1998	Devolved Scottish Parliament

SECTION 12

The Scotch Whisky Making Process and Terminology

FROM INGREDIENTS TO BOTTLE...

Whisky is made using three fundamental ingredients:

- *Scottish Water*
- *Barley or an alternative type of grain*
- *Yeast*

However, the age-old question remains—how can these three basic ingredients create a spirit that is so complex? Yet, such variations as grain, water, type of still, & cask maturation all interact to finally produce the magnificent range of aromas and taste profiles we know and love as Uisge Beatha (Gaelic for whisky or water of life).

Malting

Barley goes through the malting process to activate the enzymes which maximises the starch content. Peat is sometimes used to heat the malting floor. This can augment the smoky, peaty flavour in certain whiskies.

Mashing

The malted barley is milled to produce a course flour called *'grist'*. The grist is mixed with hot Scottish water in a mash tun. The resultant sugar laden water is known as *'wort'*. Other un-malted grains can be added at this stage if the distillery is producing blended whisky.

Fermenting

The wort is mixed with yeast and heated in a washback. The yeast feeds off the sugar in the wort, producing alcohol and carbon dioxide. This process lasts between 48 to 72hours. This is then called the *'wash'*.

Distilling:

The wash is then distilled, either using a pot or a column still. The pot still creates smaller batches whereas the column is for continuous distillation. The purpose of both is to extract alcohol spirit. Most whiskies are twice distilled.

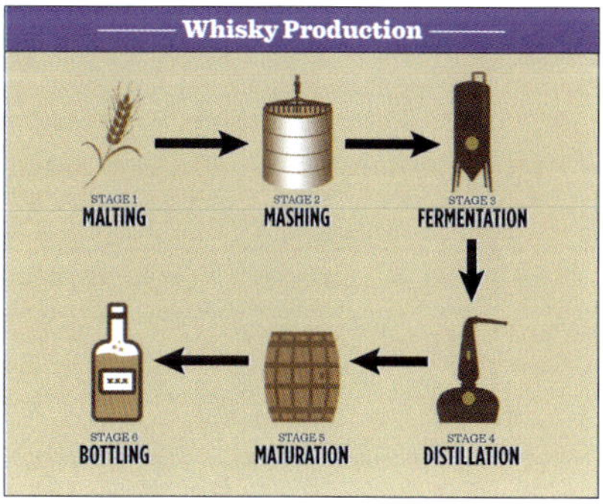

Cask Filling:

The usable spirit is now called the *'new make'*. The strength of the new make is reduced to around 64% ABV, which is ideal for maturation. The liquid is then filled into the oak casks.

Maturation:

The clear liquid slowly turns into the darker and more complex spirit in the oak casks. Maturation times can vary according to the brand of whisky. Different types of oak barrels are used to create different flavours. Generally, these barrels are ex-bourbon from the USA or ex-sherry barrels from Spain. Some whisky companies use ex-port barrels from Portugal.

Bourbon casks are said to create flavours of vanilla, caramel, sweet spice, honey and tropical fruits, whereas sherry casks are said to impart flavours of crushed almonds, golden raisins, clove, cinnamon, and citrus.

Oak casks perform three vital functions:

1. They remove the initial harshness from the new whisky

2. They add flavours such as vanilla, chocolate, dried fruit and hints of toasting

3. They allow the whisky to breathe through the cask, hence the term *'Angels Share'*

By law, all Scotch whisky must be matured for three years before being bottle and sold.

Chill Filtered

This method is used to remove residue from the whisky. The residue can cause some minor cloudiness. The whisky is cooled to between -10 and 3 degrees Centigrade. Large numbers of *'aficionado'* whisky drinkers claim this impairs the taste.

Colouring

Spirit caramel, also known as E150A, is sometimes used by some whisky distillers. This is the only substance that is legally permitted to be used in Scotch whisky.

Scotch Grain Whisky
This is distilled in a continuous still and assorted un-malted grains are utilised. Some producers market 100% grain branded whiskies. Generally, grain whiskies are cheaper to produce and are used for blending. The soft and light profiles of grain whiskies are a perfect partner with malted whisky. Many of the whisky brands on the supermarket shelves are the result of the exceptional art of blending.

The above is a very brief description on the whisky making process; you will be rewarded with a fully detailed presentation on this complex process when you visit and attend a distillery tour. These tours are very educational, fascinating and are an enjoyable experience. The whisky tasting at the end of the tour is your welcome reward for your distillery visit.

WHISKY TERMINOLOGY

ABV Alcohol by Volume

Age If an age is declared on a whisky label, ie. 10 years, that must be the youngest whisky in the blend

Angel's Share This is the evaporation of a small amount of liquid that occurs during maturation in the cask. Generally, the liquid rises to the cellar ceiling and become a stain

Batch Distillation Distillation that occurs in batches from a pot as opposed to a column still. Each batch will vary

Blended Whisky Normally, malt from a pot still and grains from a continuous still combined to create a blend

Blended Malts Blended or vatted malts are a blend of single or distillery malts

Casks These are the oak casks or barrels used to mature whisky. The barrel sizes are called *Hogshead* (250 litres), and *Butts* (500 litres). A full list of barrel sizes is shown in Section 11. Generally, they are made from US or European oak. '*Wood makes the whisky*' is an old Scottish saying

Cask Strength Usually around 56-63% ABV

Column Still Also known as the 'Coffey' or continuous still

Dram A glass of whisky, can be a quarter or fifth of a *gill* in Scotland and a sixth of a gill (2.5cl) elsewhere in the UK

Grain whisky Whisky that is made from other cereals, such as wheat and not from malted barley

Grist Ground, malted grain. Hot water is added to create a '*wash*'

Kiln An area for drying the malted barley. Smoke from peat can rise through a meshed floor and gently infuse the barley

Malt Whisky Whisky made exclusively from malted barley by double distillation in a pot still. Most malt whisky is unique and varies according to the distillery process

Malting The process of germination in a grain

Mash Tun The vessel in which the '*grist*' is mixed with hot water

Nosing Whisky is assessed by sniffing the aromas rather than tasting it

Quaich An ancient Scottish type of shallow, two-handled drinking bowl linked historically to drinking whisky. Derived from the Gaelic '*cuach*', meaning cup

Peating Adding peat to provide the heat for kiln ovens or malting floors when malting barley

Peat Reek The strength to which whisky shows smokiness in aroma and taste

Pot Still Traditionally made of copper. The still top can have various shapes

Proof The old term for the proportion of alcohol. *ABV* is the newer term

Shiel The spade used to turn barley on the malting floor

Single Cask A whisky from a single cask

Single Malt A whisky from a single distillery

Staves These are the oak planks used to create the barrel. A 200 litre barrel will have between 31 to 33 staves

Uisge Beatha The Scots Gaelic term for whisky or '*water of life*'. Pronounced "*ish – ke – ba*"

Vatting When malt whisky from different casks are mixed together

Wash The weak ale created when the '*wort*' ferments

Wort The liquid created by mixing hot water with '*grist*' in a mash tun

SECTION 13

Whisky Appreciation, Tasting and the Structural Cost of Whisky

WHISKY TASTING—SLAINTE MHATH:

1. *GLASSWARE*—It may sound obvious, but the right glass shape is crucial. You can purchase specific whisky glasses or just make sure the glass you use is similar to a red wine glass. These allows the aromas to funnel up in the glass.
2. *APPEARANCE*—Look at the hue or colour of the whisky, this can range from a light straw colour or amber to a dark gold, or light to dark brown. Swirl the whisky in the glass. Check the 'legs' inside the glass. Slow running whisky legs indicates a good body while faster running whisky indicates a thinner viscosity.
3. *AROMA ON THE NOSE*—Generally regarded as the most important factor in assessing a whisky. It generally detects more variations than the palate. Give the whisky in the glass a swirl and try to detect any aromas. Search your memory for historical aromas. Cake, dried fruit, vanilla, toast, smoke, grass, hay, cereals and a host of other aromas. If possible, try the 'memory game' and link a whisky aroma to a memorable event. A visit to the beach, on the sea, a bonfire night, a bakery shop etc. Try to write down these first impressions. Notes are vital in the overall success of a tasting.
4. *TASTE OR PALATE*—Consider the 'feel in the mouth'. Is it soft, lanolin, oily, hot, fiery, dry, tannin or lively and fresh? Again, try to record your thoughts. Consider the four primary tastes - sweetness, acidity, dryness and saltiness. This is difficult initially, but practice will make you perfect! You will get better.
5. *SCOTTISH WATER*—Add a small drop of pure still water. Repeat the 2 steps above and record the difference. Water opens a whisky to reveal even more intricate flavours. Ice tends to close down aromas.
6. *THE FINISH*—Long, medium or short? After swallowing the

whisky look for a warming glow. Sometimes the 'finish' can reveal more about a whisky's heritage and complexity. Is it dry or smooth? Or even a little harsh. Any new flavours found?

Flavours

The following flavours are associated with whisky:

- *Barley and Grains*—biscuits, porridge, bran
- *Dry or Cooked Fruit*— Either citrus, tropical, sultanas or just fruity
- *Floral*—Newly mown grass, bouquet of flowers, heather.
- *Fresh Fruit*—Apples, oranges, lemons, peaches, pears or tropical fruits.
- *Smoky*—Peat, whether in the water or in the smoke, is the main driver in the flavour. Perhaps this is the most easily recognisable flavour.
- *Medicinal*—Cough medicine, herbal remedies, disinfectant soaps etc.
- *Wood*—Recently cut, old furniture or boxes, vanilla or tannins.
- *Oily*—Lanolin, fatty or melted butter

A French perfumier once commented that he detected 26 aromas from certain Scotch whiskies!

Remember, after several swallows, your nose and palate will quickly 'numb' and it becomes increasingly more difficult to assess the whiskies. Whisky tasting is a 'sharing' activity - go to the Whisky bar, have friends around, discuss the merits of each whisky. Just enjoy!

Finally, if possible, try to mark all the above in a score from one to five, with five being the best. There is no right or wrong score. Use your own instinct and personal preferences to select an overall score. Share your score.

At the end of the HC 700 Whisky Route you will have improved your 'nose and palate'; you will also be able to discuss the merits of each whisky with other hedonistic fellow travellers.

Oh whisky! Soul o' plays an pranks!
Accept a Bardie's grateful thanks!
When wanting thee, what tuneless cranks
Are my poor verses!
Thou comes—they rattle i' their ranks
At ithers arses!

—Robert Burns

STRUCTURAL COST OF WHISKY WITH CUSTOMS DUTY AND VAT (UK)

Standard 70cl bottle of Blended Scotch @ 40% ABV

Customs Duty	**£8.04**
VAT at £15.00 RSP (UK supermarkets)	**£2.50**

So, HM Revenue & Treasury (UK government) receives a total of £10.54 on every bottle, leaving a sum of £4.46 for the actual whisky!

The following costs are involved in the delivery of your Scotch.

Cost 1—The farmer's cost of growing grain, the operating costs of a distillery, a minimum 3-year maturation period, the imported casks, the bottles and bottling, plus the packaging. Then the distillery sales and marketing, distribution and storage costs. These costs must be included in the price of a bottle of whisky, along with a commercial profit for the distillery.

Cost 2—The whisky is then provided to the supermarket, who in turn, transport to their stores. It is then placed on the shelf or delivered to your home. In addition, there must be a commercial profit for the supermarket.

The massive infrastructure involved in Cost 1 and 2 are therefore shared between the farmer, the distillery and the retailer. That leaves £4.46! In comparison a large coffee from a High Street coffee shop which is sold for around £4.00.

Therefore, approximately 70% of the sales revenue (£10.54) goes to HM Revenue & Treasury.

The selling of alcoholic spirits to the public is primarily a tax collection method.

Whisky is a *'work of passion'* for many in the industry.

Spirits, such as whisky, pay a higher amount of duty than wine, beer or cider.

The Scottish Whisky Association would welcome your views on this.

info@swa.org.uk
www.scotch-whisky.org.uk

YOUR PERSONAL WHISKY TASTING NOTES

Whisky brand			
Type			
Age		**Colour**	
Distillery			

Scoring: 1 to 5 (5 = excellent)	Points	
1. Aroma on the Nose		
2. Palate or Taste		
3. Add a small amount of water and then re-taste (no.2)		
4. Length/Finish		
5. Overall Enjoyment		
Maximum 25 points	**Total Points:**	

Slainte!

Photocopy this sheet as needed

SECTION 15

Recommended Supplementary Reading, Useful Apps, Websites and Contact addresses

WHISKY MAGAZINE

01293 312196
whiskymag@subscriptionhelpline.co.uk
https://www.whiskymag.com

By subscription.

THE SCOTCH MALT WHISKY SOCIETY

0207 831 4447
19 Greville St., Holborn, London, EC1N 8SQ

Members bars in Edinburgh, Glasgow and London.

NATIONAL TRUST FOR SCOTLAND

https://www.nts.org.uk

The NTS has a wide collection of tourist sites that are open to visitors. If you are a member, entry to all the sites is free. Annual Membership or one-time passes are available online.

SCOTTISH WHISKY ASSOCIATION

0131 222 9200
Edinburgh HQ, Quartermile Two, 2 Lister Sq. Edinburgh, EH3 9GL
info@swa.org.uk
https://www.scotch-whisky.org.uk.

VISIT SCOTLAND

VisitScotland, Ocean Point One, 94 Ocean Drive, Edinburgh, EH6 6JH
info@visitscotland.com
https://www.visitscotland.com

Visit the website for details about VisitScotland i Centres and brochures.

RNLI

Loch Ness, Scotland
lochness@rnli.org.uk

Visits are welcomed but strictly by prior appointment. Contact Joanna Stebbings at the above address to arrange a visit.

SECTION 16

20 Highland Cuisine and Fast-food Dishes

The Highlands of Scotland boast world-class food produce. Superb seafood, indigenous wild game, magnificent salmon, glorious game birds, prime beef and lamb, fresh berries and a wide selection of vegetables.

Unfortunately, items like deep fried Mars bars and Scottish tablet do tarnish the image!

Like it or loathe it, Scotland's food continues to tempt the curious and discerning visitor.

Detailed below are some samples of Scotland's foodie traditions.

1. *CULLEN SKINK*—A creamy Scottish soup, made with leeks, onions and either haddock, smoked haddock, salmon or indeed a combination of all fish. Mopped up with fresh bread is a must.

2. *BUTTERY OR BREAKFAST ROLL*—A cross between a croissant and flaky roll made with butter, lard, sugar, flour and yeast, originally conceived around Aberdeen. Add sausage or bacon as a breakfast filling. If available, try adding heather honey. Delicious.

3. *TATTIE SCONE*—Or potato scone. Best served warm or fried with a little butter.

4. *BLACK PUDDING*—Yes, the main ingredient is blood, but be brave. It is delicious.

5. *SCOTCH PIE*—A double crust pie case with minced mutton. It is the perfect 'fast food' and can be bought at any bakery or supermarket. Different fillings such as macaroni cheese, mashed potato top or with beans and mutton are available. Can be eaten hot or cold.

6. *STOVIES*—Potatoes stewed (stoved) with onions and meat. A traditional comfort food.

7. *SCOTTISH SALMON*—The wild salmon swim the North Atlantic and return to the Scottish rivers where they were born. The majority of farmed salmon is

kept in open water pens in loch inlets that have both a tidal surge combined with fresh water flowing to the sea. Smoked salmon is perfect with scrambled eggs, on its' own with some freshly baked bread not forgetting a glass of chilled white wine or malt whisky. Beautiful when it is marinaded in whisky or the regional speciality - hot smoked.

8. *BALMORAL CHICKEN*—A succulent chicken breast stuffed with haggis.

9. *CHICKEN TIKKA MASALA*—Wait! An Indian curry!? Rumour has it that it was first developed in a Glasgow Indian restaurant. Regardless of its heritage, it is one of Scotland's most popular dishes.

10. *FISH SUPPER*—A staple dish in the Scottish diet. Deep fried haddock with magnificent chips from a 'chippy'. Either with added salt and vinegar or salt and sauce? You choose!

11. *GROUSE OR PHEASANT*—The grouse is native to Scotland and has a gamey flavour while pheasants are plentiful and have adapted well to the Scottish countryside. The shooting season commences on the 12th August and concludes in December. Grouse and pheasant are delicious when casseroled or roasted. Most fine Scottish restaurants will have one or both on the menu during the season.

12. *SCOTTISH VENISON*—It is healthy, low in cholesterol and is a lean meat that shrinks little when cooked. Roe deer is available all through the year. Red deer are generally found in the west of Scotland. Venison can be cooked as a fillet or a steak. Venison casserole is equally wonderful.

Venison on the hoof

13. *HAGGIS*—Scotland's national dish, traditionally served with neeps and tatties (swede and potatoes), it is widely available and is a must on Burns Night (25th January). Myths and legends suggest Haggis was a wild animal! In fact, the 'ugly beast' is minced sheep heart, liver and lung meat with oatmeal, onions, suet, seasoning and spices. It might not sound appetising, but it is delicious and a

must try! Add a splash of whisky or whisky sauce to perfectly finish the dish.

14. ***FULL SCOTTISH FRY UP***—Fuel up for the packed day ahead. Even better after a few fine whiskies the night before. Be sure to try the square sausage and do not forget to add the haggis and black pudding.

15. ***TABLET***—Similar to fudge but made from sugar (lots), condensed milk and butter.It melts in your mouth and it will most definitely 'spike' your blood sugar levels. It is addictive! Tablet originated the 18th century.

16. ***EDINBURGH ROCK***—Different from traditional hard seaside rock—this is soft, fruity, colourful and crumbly.

17. ***SHORTBREAD***—Made from flour, sugar and butter. A rich, crumbly, buttery biscuit, perfect with a cup of tea. Available In packets and tins. A wonderful gift for when you return home.

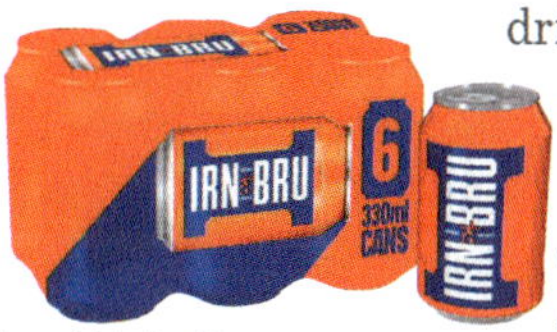

The mighty Irn-Bru

18. ***TUNNOCK'S TEA CAKES***—A small round biscuit with a dome of marshmallow and covered in chocolate. Iconic red and silver foil wrapping. Ideal snack with tea or coffee.

19. ***SCOTTISH CHEESE BOARD***—The unique climate means that a full range of cheeses from Cheddar to the soft and creamy variety. Orkney makes wonderful smoked cheeses. It is worth seeking out Crowdie, a soft cheese introduced by the Vikings. Caboc, said to be Scotland's oldest cheese originating from the 14th Century - the cheese is rolled in toasted pin head oatmeal. Enjoy Highland brie or if you prefer blue cheese, try Blue Murder! Cheese can be enjoyed with Scottish Oatcakes.

20. ***CRANACHAN***—The king of desserts in Scotland. It combines cream, raspberries and oat flakes or pin head oats.

And not forgetting the non-alcoholic drink that symbolises Scotland in a can, **IRN-BRU**.

Truly delightful with fish and chips and a refreshing change to the duopoly of Coke and Pepsi.

SECTION 17

Road Safety and Driving in the Scottish Highlands and Islands

LET'S BE CAREFUL OUT THERE...

- A vitally important point to remember is that Scotland's drink and driving rules are stricter that the rest of the UK and many other international countries. The limit is as follows:
  22 micrograms (mcg) of alcohol in 100ml of breath.

- Depending on age, size, time of last meal, etc, one alcoholic drink could put you over the limit.

- Take your time on the HC 700 Whisky Route. Many of the viewing places are wonderful, breath-taking and stunningly glorious. The spectacular sunsets on the West Coast are awesome. The sunrises on the East Coast are equally enthralling. Please remember other people are using the route so take care and display courtesy.

- Other users on the route include walkers, hikers, cyclists, motorcyclists, cars with and without caravans, camper vans and large lorries, not forgetting agricultural equipment and vehicles such as tractors. Children require special attention. All are entitled to the joys and safety of this route. Please therefore share the road sensibly.

- Passing places can be an inconvenience but are a necessity. Stay aware to the different driving skills needed on these challenging roads.

- Stay within the speed limits, particularly by schools.

- There will be sheep, cattle, deer, other wild animals as well as domestic pets on the route. Please drive carefully when you pass animals. Slow movements with no car horn are best. Hitting a large animal, such as a deer can be catastrophic for both animal and car occupants.

Highland cows

- Ensure your vehicle is in good condition and it is advisable to have some form of emergency breakdown service, such as the AA or RAC.
- Finally, always follow the Highway Code rules and please apply common sense and safety at ALL times.

ALWAYS DRINK RESPONSIBLY

SECTION 18

Please Follow the Countryside Code

COMMON SENSE AND COURTESY IS ALWAYS BEST...

- Always ask permission (if possible) when entering fenced areas and agricultural land. Try to keep to paths and tracks.
- Ensure you close all country gates after use.
- Do not disturb livestock.
- Dogs must always be on a lead. Farmers are vigilant about dogs worrying sheep and cattle.
- Please take all your litter, bottles and general rubbish to an appropriate rubbish bin. Do not light fires in the dry summer months.
- Always drive with care, especially where animals may be. Highland roads can be narrow and difficult to negotiate.
- Be extremely careful near cliffs and on mountainous areas, especially if you have children. Extra care should be taken if you decide to swim in lochs, rivers or in the sea. The water can be bitterly cold, tides and currents can be dangerous.
- Be careful around animals, especially those close to their young. Cattle should be avoided. Be considerate near birds, particularly when they are nesting.
- If you decide to go for a longer walk, please ensure you have the appropriate waterproof clothes and boots. Remember, not all areas have a mobile phone signal. In the winter months, take a torch, food and water with you. The wintry weather in the Highlands is notorious and can change from calm to a stormy blizzard with torrential rain in a relatively short time. Finally,leave a note in the car or tell somebody your plans and timing.

SCOTTISH OUTDOOR ACCESS CODE
outdooraccess-scotland.scot

SECTION 19

HC 700 Photographic Competition 2021

The glens, lochs, castles, mountains, wild coasts, sunrises, sunsets, the whiskies, the distilleries and the rugged scenery all combine to provide the perfect backdrop for that special photograph. Wildlife, people and friends can also provide fascinating photos.

So many superb photo opportunities, not forgetting the humorous or simply 'I have been there' photos are taken every year. They deserve to be shared with fellow or future HC 700 travellers.

So, between the months of May and October 2021 we will ask you to email your special photos to Spirit of the Glen Ltd at:

info@HC700.com

The winning photo each month will be presented with a bottle of Slainte HC 700 Highland Single Malt Whisky, delivered to their UK home. All entrants must be over 18 to enter the competition. The winners will be advised each month.

A selection of received photos will be shown on the HC 700 website.

To enter:

Simply email your photo/s with location and other pertinent details to info@HC700.com. A maximum of two photos per person. Go on, be creative, and enjoy sharing your photographs on the HC 700 website.

Good Luck to you—Gur math a theid leat

WE'RE GOOD TO GO
ESTD 1897
TOMATIN
DISTILLERY
Scottish
TOURIST BOARD
★★★★
VISITOR ATTRACTION
EXPERIENCE THE 'SOFTER SIDE OF THE HIGHLANDS' AT TOMATIN DISTILLERY WITH A QUALITY RANGE OF TOURS & AWARD WINNING WHISKIES AVAILABLE
OPENING TIMES: THE COVID RESTRICTIONS MEAN THESE ARE SUBJECT TO CHANGE. PLEASE VISIT: WWW.TOMATIN.COM/VISIT FOR LATEST INFORMATION
VISIT OUR ONLINE SHOP - WWW.TOMATINDISTILLERY.SHOP
TOMATIN, INVERNESS-SHIRE, IV13 7YT
TEL: 01463 248 144 EMAIL: VISITORS@TOMATIN.COM

SECTION 20

Scottish HC 700 Passport

CONDITIONS ON THE ISSUE OF A HC 700 CERTIFICATE

- You must have at least three distillery visits with a distillery stamp or a copy of the Visitor Centre receipt.
- Official HC 700 stamps are available at *Castle Tavern,* or any of the Whisky bars in Inverness, *Carnegie Cellars in Dornoch*, a copy of the Orkney Ferry receipt, *Torridon Hotel, Royal Hotel or Whisky bar* in Ullapool, *Cuillins Hotel (Whisky bar or View Restaurant)* Skye, or the *Loch Ness Monster Centre* or *Clansman Hotel* or Gift Shop, Drumnadrochit
- Only six stamps required
- HC 700 Passport and copies of supporting receipts should be sent to: Spirit of the Glen Ltd., Ilex House, 48 Ash Lane, Rustington, BN16 3BT or to info@HC700.com
- The official HC 700 Certificate will be emailed or posted.

Slàinte
Whisky & Tartan
Highland Coast
whisky route
"Spirit of the Glen"
Loch Ness
MacDonald Tartan
Slàinte
Scots Gaelic—*Good health* or *Cheers*
A HIGHLAND SINGLE MALT WHISKY FOR YOUR SIPPING ENJOYMENT
Complex, yet true in spirit—Mellow, yet with attitude
The Scottish Highlands yet in a glass...
Slàinte mhath!
Order a bottle of HC 700 or ask for your personal Malt Whisky label—our speciality
Inver Associates Ltd.
07427 909906
sales@inverspirits.com
www.inverspirits.com

Notes

Printed in Great Britain
by Amazon

63318609R00052